Unlocking Your Desires

How to Get Exactly What You Want

By

Dick P. Blair

Table of contents

Introduction

In the pursuit of a fulfilling and satisfying life, it is only natural to have desires. These desires often stem from the deepest recesses of our hearts and minds, representing our true aspirations and dreams. Whether it's achieving professional success, nurturing meaningful relationships, attaining financial abundance, or experiencing personal growth, our desires act as guiding beacons, directing us towards a life of purpose and contentment. However, the process of realizing our desires is not always straightforward. We encounter obstacles, face self-doubt, and may find ourselves caught in the trap of unfulfilled wishes.

But what if there was a way to unlock the power within us and manifest exactly what we want? What if we could learn the art of bringing our desires to life, effectively transforming our dreams into reality? This book is dedicated to exploring precisely that.

Throughout this book, we will delve into the depths of desire, understanding its significance and unraveling the secrets to its manifestation. We will embark on a transformative journey together, uncovering the tools, techniques, and mindset required to align our desires with our actions, ultimately unlocking the doors to a life that mirrors our deepest longings.

Desires are not mere whims or passing fancies; they are the whispers of our soul, calling us to explore our fullest potential. They possess the power to ignite passion, fuel motivation, and inspire us to embark on extraordinary paths. However, many individuals struggle to identify their true desires, clouded by societal expectations or their own self-imposed limitations. This book aims to guide you through the process of self-discovery, helping you unlock the doors to your authentic desires.

As we embark on this journey, it is essential to recognize that the process of getting exactly what we want is multifaceted. It requires a holistic approach that encompasses various aspects of our lives, from setting clear and compelling goals to cultivating a positive mindset to taking inspired action to building supportive relationships. Each step in this process plays a vital role in shaping our reality and propelling us closer to the fulfillment of our desires.

We will explore the power of visualization, affirmations, and intention setting, learning how to harness these tools to create a vivid mental image of our desires and program our minds for success. We will also delve into the art of crafting meaningful goals, ensuring they are specific, measurable, achievable, relevant, and time-bound (S.M.A.R.T.), thus setting ourselves up for success.

Moreover, we will address the internal barriers that often stand in the way of manifesting our desires. Limiting beliefs, fear, and self-doubt can be formidable obstacles that hinder our progress. By identifying these obstacles and implementing strategies to overcome them, we can break free from their grip and move forward with unwavering confidence.

Taking inspired action is a crucial component of the journey toward getting what we want. It is not enough to simply dream and visualize; we must translate our desires into tangible steps and actively pursue them. This book will provide guidance on creating action plans, staying motivated, and overcoming the inevitable challenges that arise along the way.

Recognizing the importance of external support, we will explore the significance of nurturing a supportive environment. Building a network of positive influences, seeking accountability partners, and surrounding ourselves with like-minded individuals can greatly enhance our ability to manifest our desires. Together, we will learn how to create a physical and emotional space that supports our aspirations and encourages our growth.

Furthermore, we will embrace the notion that setbacks and challenges are not roadblocks but rather opportunities for growth. By adopting a growth mindset, we can view setbacks as valuable lessons that propel us forward. Resilience, adaptability, and the ability to extract wisdom from adversity will be essential tools in our arsenal as we journey toward the fulfillment of our desires.

Throughout this book, we will emphasize the power of gratitude and celebration. Cultivating gratitude for what we have and celebrating our milestones and achievements are essential practices that fuel our progress and enhance our sense of fulfillment.

Now, dear reader, it is time to embark on this transformative voyage of self-discovery and manifestation. By delving into the depths of your desires and aligning your actions with your authentic aspirations, you will embark on a path that leads to the fulfillment of your dreams. Together, let us unlock the power within and learn how to get exactly what we want.

Chapter 1

Understanding Desires and Their Importance

Desires are the driving forces that propel us forward, urging us to pursue our dreams, fulfill our aspirations, and seek a life of meaning and fulfillment. They are the inner yearnings that reside within us, representing our deepest wants and longings

To truly understand desires, we must first recognize their multifaceted nature. Desires encompass a wide spectrum of human experiences and can manifest in various aspects of our lives. They can be related to our careers, relationships, personal growth, health, creativity, or any other area that holds significance for us. Each desire represents a unique facet of our individuality, reflecting our values, passions, and aspirations.

Desires act as compasses, guiding us towards a life that aligns with our true selves. They provide us with a sense of purpose and direction, offering a vision of the life we wish to create. When we acknowledge and honor our desires, we embark on a path of self-discovery and self-actualization. Our desires act as beacons, illuminating the way and helping us navigate the vast sea of possibilities.

In a society that often imposes external expectations and norms upon us, it is essential to distinguish our authentic desires from the desires of others. We must peel away the layers of societal conditioning and delve deep into our hearts and minds to unearth our true desires. This requires self-reflection, introspection, and the courage to challenge societal expectations. By doing so, we reclaim our autonomy and pave the way for a life that is true to ourselves.

The importance of understanding our desires cannot be overstated. When we are in touch with our deepest longings, we gain clarity and focus. Our desires become the driving force behind our actions, motivating us to pursue our goals with unwavering determination. Without a clear understanding of our desires, we risk drifting aimlessly, feeling unfulfilled and disconnected from our true purpose.

Moreover, desires serve as catalysts for personal growth and transformation. They beckon us to step out of our comfort zones, embrace challenges, and stretch our capabilities. Pursuing our desires often involves taking risks and facing uncertainty, but it is through these experiences that we learn, evolve, and become the best versions of ourselves. Our desires become vehicles for self-discovery, allowing us to explore our strengths, talents, and untapped potential.

Desires also infuse our lives with passion and enthusiasm. When we are aligned with our desires, we approach our endeavors with a sense of joy, zest, and vitality. Our work becomes more fulfilling, our relationships more meaningful, and our overall experience of life more vibrant. Desires bring a sense of purpose and excitement, igniting a fire within us that fuels our journey.

In addition to their personal impact, desires also have a collective significance. When individuals are in touch with their authentic desires and actively pursue them, they contribute to the fabric of society. The pursuit of desires often leads to innovation, creativity, and positive change. Individuals who are aligned with their desires tend to make valuable contributions to their communities, uplift others, and inspire those around them to live authentically.

It is important to note that desires are not static entities. They evolve and transform as we grow, gain new experiences, and gain deeper insights into ourselves. Our desires may shift, expand, or refine over time, reflecting our evolving values, priorities, and aspirations. Therefore, it is crucial to engage in an ongoing process of self-reflection and introspection to stay connected with our desires and ensure they continue to align with our authentic selves.

In summary, desires are the driving forces that propel us towards a life of meaning, purpose, and fulfillment. They represent our true aspirations, values, and passions. Understanding our desires and acknowledging their importance is the first step towards unlocking their transformative power. When we embrace our desires, align our actions with them, and navigate our lives with clarity and intention, we embark on a journey of self-discovery and self-actualization. The journey towards understanding and fulfilling our desires is not always easy, but it is undoubtedly worth the effort, as it leads us to a life that is rich, meaningful, and deeply fulfilling.

Defining Desires: Unveiling Your Inner Passions

Desires are the heart's whispers, the inner longings that stir our souls and drive us towards a life of purpose and fulfillment. They represent our deepest yearnings, reflecting the essence of who we are and what we truly value. In this chapter, we will embark on a journey of self-discovery, exploring the process of defining desires and uncovering our inner passions.

1. The Essence of Desires

Desires are not fleeting whims or superficial wants; they go far deeper than that. They tap into the core of our being, resonating with our authentic selves. Desires are the language of the soul, expressing our unique preferences, dreams, and aspirations. They reflect what truly matters to us, what brings us joy, and what gives our lives meaning.

Understanding desires requires us to look beyond societal expectations and external influences. It involves peeling away the layers of conditioning, assumptions, and fears that may have clouded our vision of what we truly want. It requires the courage to be honest with ourselves and the willingness to embrace our genuine desires, even if they diverge from conventional norms.

2. Self-Reflection and Introspection

Defining desires begins with self-reflection and introspection. Taking the time to pause, step back, and examine our inner landscape allows us to connect with our true selves and explore the depths of our desires. Here are some valuable practices to facilitate this process:

Journaling: Writing down our thoughts, feelings, and aspirations can provide clarity and insights into our desires. Journaling allows us to explore our passions, interests, and values, helping us uncover the underlying desires that drive us.

Mindfulness and Meditation: Cultivating mindfulness and engaging in meditation practices create space for self-awareness and introspection. By quieting the mind and observing our thoughts and emotions, we can gain valuable insights into our deepest desires

Questioning Assumptions: Challenging the assumptions we have about ourselves and our desires is a crucial step. Often, we inherit beliefs or adopt societal expectations that may not align with our true desires. By questioning these assumptions, we can uncover our authentic passions.

3. Exploring Passions and Interests

Passions and interests act as gateways to our desires. They provide clues about what truly excites us, brings us joy, and captivates our attention. Exploring our passions allows us to dive deeper into our desires and connect with the activities and experiences that align with our authentic selves.

Childhood Reflection: Recalling the activities and interests we were naturally drawn to as children can reveal our innate passions. Reflecting on these early inclinations can help us reconnect with the desires we may have set aside or forgotten over time.

Curiosity and Experimentation: Cultivating curiosity and a spirit of experimentation enables us to explore new interests and activities. Trying out different hobbies, attending workshops, or engaging in diverse experiences can help us uncover hidden passions and desires.

Paying Attention to Energy and Excitement: Observing the activities that energize us and evoke a sense of excitement is another way to uncover our desires. When we engage in activities that bring us joy and enthusiasm, it often indicates alignment with our authentic desires.

4. Values and Core Beliefs

Desires are closely intertwined with our values and core beliefs. Identifying and understanding these foundational elements provides valuable insights into our desires and aspirations. Our values act as guiding principles, shaping our choices and influencing our desires. Exploring our values helps us understand what truly matters to us and what we seek to manifest in our lives.

Values Clarification: Reflecting on the values that resonate deeply with us allows us to uncover desires that align with those values. Whether it's integrity, creativity, compassion, or freedom, our desires are often an expression of our core values.

Personal Mission Statement: Creating a personal mission statement can help distill our values and desires into a concise statement that acts as a compass for our lives. Articulating our mission provides clarity and direction, guiding us towards the fulfillment of our desires.

5. Embracing Authenticity and Overcoming Fear

Defining desires requires authenticity and courage. It involves embracing our true selves, even if it means venturing into uncharted territory or facing potential judgment. Authenticity liberates us from the expectations of others and empowers us to embrace our desires with conviction.

Letting Go of Fear: Fear can often hinder the process of defining desires. The fear of failure, rejection, or judgment may prevent us from acknowledging and pursuing our deepest desires. By recognizing and releasing these fears, we create space for our authentic desires to emerge.

Embracing Vulnerability: Defining desires requires vulnerability—a willingness to open ourselves up to the possibilities and potential disappointments that come with pursuing our passions. Embracing vulnerability allows us to fully connect with our desires and express them authentically.

Defining desires is a deeply personal and transformative process. It requires self-reflection, introspection, and the courage to embrace our authentic selves. By exploring our passions, values, and beliefs, we unlock the gateways to our desires. In doing so, we step onto a path that leads to a life aligned with our deepest longings—a life of purpose, fulfillment, and authenticity.

Recognizing the Power of Desires in Shaping Your Life

Desires are not mere whims or passing fancies; they possess an inherent power that can shape the trajectory of our lives. They act as catalysts for growth, transformation, and the pursuit of personal fulfillment.

1. The Driving Force of Desires

Desires serve as powerful driving forces that propel us forward on our life's path. They fuel our ambition, inspire our actions, and provide the necessary motivation to overcome challenges and obstacles. Desires create a sense of purpose and direction, giving us a destination to strive for and a vision to manifest.

When we tap into the power of desires, we awaken a deep reservoir of energy and passion within us. Our desires become the fuel that ignites our creativity, determination, and perseverance. They infuse our actions with meaning, allowing us to fully engage in the pursuit of our goals and dreams.

2. Unleashing Potential and Possibility

Desires are the seeds of potential and possibility. They awaken dormant talents, strengths, and abilities within us, urging us to explore our full potential. When we align our actions with our desires, we tap into a wellspring of creativity, innovation, and personal growth.

By embracing our desires, we unlock doors to new opportunities and experiences. Our desires push us beyond our comfort zones, compelling us to step into the unknown and embrace the challenges that come with growth. Through this process, we discover capabilities and talents we may have never realized we possessed.

3. Creating a Sense of Meaning and Fulfillment

Desires provide a sense of meaning and fulfillment in our lives. When we pursue our deepest desires, we engage in activities and experiences that resonate with our core values, passions, and aspirations. This alignment brings a profound sense of purpose and satisfaction, enriching our daily lives and giving us a deeper sense of fulfillment.

Living a life guided by desires allows us to create a meaningful narrative. Each desire fulfilled becomes a chapter in our personal story, building a tapestry of experiences that reflect our journey of growth, purpose, and self-discovery. By honoring our desires, we create a life that is true to ourselves and aligned with our authentic selves.

4. Inspiring Growth and Personal Development

Desires act as catalysts for personal growth and development. They push us to expand our boundaries, learn new skills, and overcome self-imposed limitations. Pursuing our desires requires continuous growth as we strive to acquire the knowledge, resources, and abilities necessary to manifest our dreams.

The pursuit of desires also fosters resilience and adaptability. As we encounter obstacles and setbacks, we learn to navigate challenges, persevere in the face of adversity, and adapt our strategies. Through this process, we develop invaluable skills and qualities that strengthen our character and enable us to overcome future obstacles.

5. Harnessing Emotional Alignment and Well-being

When our desires align with our values, passions, and purpose, we experience a deep sense of emotional alignment and well-being. The pursuit of desires brings joy, enthusiasm, and a sense of vitality to our lives. It creates a state of flow, where time seems to disappear as we engage in activities that align with our deepest longings.

By acknowledging and honoring our desires, we cultivate a positive emotional state. We experience a sense of fulfillment and satisfaction as we make progress towards our goals. This positive emotional state enhances our overall well-being, contributing to increased happiness, self-confidence, and a positive outlook on life.

6. Inspiring Others and Making a Difference

Our desires have the power to inspire and impact the lives of others. When we live authentically and pursue our passions, we become a source of inspiration and motivation for those around us. Our commitment to our desires can ignite the flame of possibility in others, encouraging them to pursue their own dreams and desires.

By embracing our desires and manifesting them in the world, we contribute to the collective consciousness. Our actions, fueled by desires, have the potential to create positive change, influence our communities, and make a difference in the lives of others. The power of desires extends beyond our individual lives, reaching out to touch the lives of those we encounter.

Embracing the Value of Fulfilling Your Desires

Satisfying our desires is a strong and groundbreaking experience that enhances our lives in various ways. It is a demonstration of self-strengthening, a statement of our value, and a pledge to carry on with an existence of direction and legitimacy. In this part, we will investigate the benefits of satisfying our longings and how they contribute to our general prosperity, development, and satisfaction.

1. Honoring Your Authentic Self

Satisfying our desires is a demonstration of our authentic selves. It is an acknowledgment that our cravings are substantial, significant, and deserving of pursuit. At the point when we embrace the benefit of satisfying our longings, we recognize that our fantasies and goals matter and that we have the right to carry on with a day-to-day existence that lines up with our actual embodiment.

By respecting our valid selves and satisfying our longings, we develop profound identity acknowledgment and self-esteem. We let go of cultural assumptions and outer approval, and we embrace our special ways and distinctions. This demonstration of self-respect is a strong step towards self-completion and individual satisfaction.

2. Living with Enthusiasm and Reason

Satisfying our cravings permits us to live with energy and reason. At the point when we participate in exercises, pursuits, and connections that line up with our most profound longings, we implant our lives with a sense of significance and imperativeness. We awaken every day with a feeling of energy and excitement, realizing that our activities are in harmony with our interests and values.

Living with enthusiasm and reason upgrades our general prosperity. It builds our inspiration, energy levels, and commitment to life. We feel a more noteworthy sense of fulfillment and satisfaction in our day-to-day encounters, as we are effectively adding to the sign of our cravings.

3. Expanding Your Comfort Zone

Satisfying our longings requires us to step beyond our usual range of familiarity. It pushes us to embrace vulnerability, face challenges, and adventure into the unexplored world. By extending our usual range of familiarity, we free ourselves up to new encounters, open doors, and self-improvement.

Venturing beyond our usual range of familiarity encourages flexibility, versatility, and self-improvement. It provokes us to face fears, defeat impediments, and foster new abilities and qualities. Each time we satisfy a longing that takes us past our usual range of familiarity, we extend our capacities and construct trust in our capacity to explore the difficulties that emerge on our excursion.

4. Cultivating a Positive Mindset

Satisfying our longings sustains a positive outlook. It includes developing confidence, self-conviction, and faith in the overflow of potential outcomes. At the point when we embrace the benefit of satisfying our cravings, we shift our concentration from impediments to open doors, from hindrances to arrangements. This positive mentality empowers us to move toward difficulties with strength, inventiveness, and assurance.

Cultivating a positive outlook improves our general prosperity and psychological wellness. It works on our capacity to adapt to pressure, builds our self-assurance, and cultivates a more prominent feeling of joy and satisfaction. A positive outlook turns into the establishment whereupon we construct the existence of our fantasies.

5. Motivating Others

At the point when we satisfy our longings, we rouse others to do likewise. Our activities act as a demonstration of the force of dreams, the chance of individual change, and the quest for a significant life. By living in accordance with our cravings, we become reference points of motivation, propelling others to take advantage of their own longings and make strides towards their satisfaction.

Moving others is a significant method for adding to the prosperity of our networks and society overall. By exemplifying the benefit of satisfying our cravings, we urge others to embrace their legitimate selves, follow their interests, and make positive change in their lives. Our satisfaction turns into a far-reaching influence that spreads a long way beyond our singular process.

6. Cultivating Gratitude and Appreciation

Satisfying our longings develops a profound sense of gratitude and appreciation. It permits us to perceive and praise the favors and accomplishments in our lives. At the point when we satisfy a longing, we experience a significant feeling of appreciation for the excursion that drove us there, the examples advanced en route, and the help we got.

Rehearsing gratitude and appreciation improves our general prosperity. It moves our concentration from the thing that is missing to what is bountiful in our lives. Appreciation opens our hearts, builds our joy, and develops our association with ourselves as well as other people. By satisfying our longings and developing appreciation, we create a positive criticism circle that further improves our capacity to draw in and manifest our fantasies.

Embracing the benefit of satisfying our longings is a groundbreaking and engaging decision. It respects our credible selves, implants our lives with enthusiasm and reason, and grows our usual range of familiarity. It develops a positive outlook, motivates others, and encourages gratitude and appreciation. Satisfying our longings isn't just an individual demonstration of self-strengthening; it likewise adds to the shared mindset, motivating others to embrace their own cravings and carry on with lives of validness, satisfaction, and bliss. By embracing the benefit of satisfying our longings, we set out on an excursion of self-disclosure, development, and extreme satisfaction.

Chapter 2

Discovering Your Authentic Desires

Our authentic desires hold the key to a life of purpose, fulfillment, and joy. They represent the truest expressions of who we are, reflecting our deepest longings, passions, and aspirations. Together we will embark on a journey of self-discovery, exploring the process of uncovering our authentic desires and aligning our lives with what truly matters to us.

1. Unveiling the Layers

Discovering our authentic desires requires peeling away the layers of conditioning, expectations, and societal influences that may have clouded our vision of what we truly want. It involves unraveling the beliefs, fears, and limitations that may have held us back from acknowledging our deepest longings. To embark on this journey, we must create space for self-reflection, introspection, and honest exploration.

2. Embracing Self-Reflection

Self-reflection is a powerful tool for uncovering our authentic desires. It involves setting aside time to connect with our inner selves, to examine our thoughts, feelings, and experiences, and to explore the questions that reside deep within us. Here are some practices to cultivate self-reflection:

Mindfulness and Meditation: Cultivating mindfulness and engaging in meditation practices allows us to quiet the mind, observe our thoughts and emotions, and gain insight into our true desires. By being present and aware of our inner experiences, we can uncover the whispers of our soul.

Journaling: Writing in a journal provides a safe space for self-expression and exploration. Through journaling, we can delve into our thoughts, emotions, and experiences, gaining clarity and uncovering patterns and themes that reveal our authentic desires.

Solitude and Silence: Creating moments of solitude and silence allows us to disconnect from external distractions and tune into our inner wisdom. By embracing moments of quiet contemplation, we can access the voice of our intuition and uncover our deepest desires.

3. Trusting Your Intuition

Our intuition is a powerful guide for discovering our authentic desires. It is the subtle inner voice that whispers truths and nudges us in the direction of our deepest longings. To tap into our intuition, we must learn to trust ourselves and listen to the quiet whispers of our hearts.

Trusting our intuition involves cultivating self-trust, letting go of self-doubt, and embracing the notion that we possess wisdom and guidance within us. It requires creating space for stillness, listening to our inner knowing, and honoring the messages that arise from deep within.

4. Identifying Values and Passions

Our values and passions provide valuable clues to uncovering our authentic desires. Our values represent what is most important to us, while our passions ignite our enthusiasm and bring us joy. Exploring these aspects of ourselves allows us to connect with the desires that align with our truest selves.

Values Clarification: Reflecting on our core values helps us identify the desires that are in alignment with what we hold dear. Whether it is love, freedom, growth, or contribution, our desires often spring from the well of our values.

Passion Exploration: Exploring our passions, interests, and activities that bring us joy helps us uncover desires that are rooted in our authentic selves. Engaging in activities that captivate our attention and excite our hearts provides valuable insights into our deepest longings.

5. Paying Attention to Emotional Signals

Our emotions are powerful indicators of our desires. They act as signals, guiding us towards what brings us joy, fulfillment, and a sense of aliveness. Paying attention to our emotional responses and reactions helps us uncover desires that resonate deeply within us.

When we feel a surge of joy, enthusiasm, or excitement, it often signifies alignment with our authentic desires. On the other hand, feelings of discontent, frustration, or apathy may indicate a misalignment with our true desires. By tuning into our emotional landscape, we can gain clarity on what truly matters to us and what we yearn to manifest in our lives.

6. Embracing Curiosity and Exploration

Curiosity and exploration are essential ingredients in the process of discovering our authentic desires. By adopting a mindset of openness and a willingness to try new experiences, we expand our horizons and create opportunities for self-discovery.

Embracing curiosity involves asking ourselves questions such as "What if?" or "What truly excites me?" It entails stepping outside our comfort zones, trying new activities, and venturing into uncharted territories. Through this exploration, we encounter experiences, people, and opportunities that shed light on our authentic desires.

7. Embodying Authenticity

Discovering our authentic desires requires embracing our true selves and expressing our desires authentically. It involves letting go of the need for external validation and embracing our uniqueness and individuality.

To embody authenticity, we must release the fear of judgment and embrace vulnerability. It is through embracing our authentic selves that we create a life that is true to our desires. By living in alignment with our truest selves, we inspire others to do the same, creating a ripple effect of authenticity and empowerment.

Discovering our authentic desires is a deeply personal and transformative journey. It requires self-reflection, trust in our intuition, exploration of values and passions, attention to emotional signals, and a curiosity-driven mindset. By peeling away the layers of conditioning and embracing our true selves, we uncover desires that align with our deepest longings, passions, and aspirations. Embracing our authentic desires empowers us to live a life of purpose, fulfillment, and joy—a life that is in alignment with our truest selves.

Self-Reflection: Exploring Your Innermost Desires

Self-reflection is a powerful practice that allows us to delve into the depths of our being, to explore our thoughts, emotions, and experiences, and to gain insight into our true desires. It is a journey of self-discovery that uncovers the whispers of our soul and illuminates the path towards our deepest longings. In this chapter, we will explore the practice of self-reflection and how it can lead us to explore and understand our innermost desires.

1. The Practice of Self-Reflection

Self-reflection is a process of introspection and examination of our inner world. It involves setting aside dedicated time and creating a safe space for deep self-inquiry. Through self-reflection, we gain a deeper understanding of our thoughts, feelings, beliefs, values, and desires.

The practice of self-reflection can take many forms, such as journaling, meditation, mindfulness, or engaging in creative activities. The key is to create a space for stillness and silence where we can connect with our inner selves without distractions. By embracing self-reflection, we embark on a transformative journey of self-discovery, paving the way for the exploration of our innermost desires.

2. Cultivating Awareness

Self-reflection begins with cultivating awareness. It is about becoming fully present and attentive to our thoughts, emotions, sensations, and experiences. Cultivating awareness allows us to observe ourselves without judgment, curiosity, or openness.

By becoming aware of our inner landscape, we gain insights into the patterns, beliefs, and conditioning that may have influenced our desires. We start to unravel the layers that may have obscured our authentic desires, and we create space for new possibilities to emerge. Cultivating awareness is the foundation upon which the exploration of our innermost desires is built.

3. Connecting with Your Heart's Whispers

The practice of self-reflection enables us to connect with the whispers of our hearts—the innermost desires that lie deep within us. It is in the stillness and silence of self-reflection that these desires can emerge and be heard. By creating space for self-reflection, we invite our desires to surface, guiding us towards a life that aligns with our truest selves.

Listening to our hearts whispers requires attunement and receptivity. It involves tuning into our intuition, that subtle inner voice that speaks the language of our desires. Through self-reflection, we learn to trust and honor these whispers, even if they challenge societal norms or go against external expectations.

4. Exploring Core Needs and Desires

Self-reflection allows us to explore our core needs and desires—the fundamental aspects that shape our experience of life. By understanding our core needs, we gain clarity on the desires that arise from these needs and the actions required to fulfill them.

Exploring our core needs involves reflecting on areas such as security, connection, belonging, growth, autonomy, and self-expression. By examining these needs, we can identify the desires that are aligned with fulfilling them. For example, a need for connection may lead to a desire for nurturing relationships, while a need for growth may manifest as a desire for personal development and learning.

5. Questioning Assumptions and Conditioning

Self-reflection challenges the assumptions and conditioning that may have influenced our desires. It invites us to question the beliefs, expectations, and narratives that we have inherited or adopted. By critically examining these assumptions, we free ourselves from limitations and open the door to exploring our authentic desires.

Questioning assumptions involves asking ourselves thought-provoking questions, such as:

"Whose desires am I truly pursuing?"

"What societal expectations have influenced my desires?"

"Are my desires in alignment with my values and true self?"

"What fears or limiting beliefs are holding me back from acknowledging my authentic desires?"

By challenging assumptions, we create space for our genuine desires to emerge and guide us towards a life of authenticity and fulfillment.

Uncovering Desires Beyond Societal Expectations

Self-reflection allows us to uncover desires that go beyond societal expectations or external influences. It frees us from the pressure to conform and invites us to explore our unique longings and aspirations.

By examining the desires that may have been suppressed or dismissed due to societal norms, we reclaim our autonomy and honor our individuality. Self-reflection liberates us from the need for approval and empowers us to embrace desires that are true to ourselves, even if they deviate from societal expectations.

1. Embracing the Uncomfortable

Self-reflection is not always comfortable. It requires courage to explore our inner world and confront aspects of ourselves that may be challenging or uncomfortable. However, it is in these moments of discomfort that the greatest growth and self-discovery can occur.

By embracing the uncomfortable, we expand our capacity for self-awareness, acceptance, and transformation. The exploration of our innermost desires may bring forth emotions, fears, or vulnerabilities, but it is through embracing these aspects that we truly connect with our authentic desires and embark on a journey of self-actualization.

2. Taking Inspired Action

Self-reflection is not solely an intellectual exercise; it is a call to action. It inspires us to take steps towards manifesting our desires in the physical world. Through self-reflection, we gain clarity on the actions required to fulfill our desires, and we cultivate the motivation and determination to pursue them.

Taking inspired action means aligning our thoughts, intentions, and behaviors with our authentic desires. It involves setting goals, creating action plans, and embracing the courage to step into the unknown. By integrating self-reflection with intentional action, we bridge the gap between our innermost desires and their manifestation in our lives.

Self-reflection is a powerful practice that allows us to explore our innermost desires. It cultivates awareness, connects us with our hearts whispers, and challenges assumptions and conditioning. Through self-reflection, we uncover desires that are authentic, aligned with our core needs, and free from societal expectations. By embracing self-reflection, we embark on a transformative journey of self-discovery.

3. Uncovering Desires Beyond Societal Expectations

Societal expectations play a huge part in forming our desires. Since early on, we have been affected by social standards, media depictions, and the strain to adjust to specific beliefs. These outside impacts can cloud our real cravings and lead us to seek after yearnings that may not genuinely line up with what our identity is. In this section, we will investigate the significance of uncovering past cultural assumptions and embracing our most genuine longings.

The Impact of Societal Expectations

Societal expectations penetrate each part of our lives. They direct what achievement resembles, what connections ought to be like, and the way that we ought to introduce ourselves to the world. These expectations create a structure inside which we frequently shape our cravings, sometimes without acknowledging it.

By adjusting to societal expectations, we might wind up seeking after wants that are not genuinely our own. We might focus on outer markers of accomplishment or adjust to cultural standards, regardless of whether they resonate with our credible selves. In doing so, we risk forfeiting our real cravings and undermining our own satisfaction.

4. The Significance of Realness

Uncovering past cultural assumptions starts with embracing realness. Legitimacy is the act of being consistent with oneself and respecting our special personalities, values, and wants. It is an extreme demonstration of self-acknowledgment and self-articulation that liberates us from the limits of cultural standards.

At the point when we embrace legitimacy, we free ourselves from the requirement for outside approval. We permit our actual longings to arise and direct us towards a daily existence that mirrors our certified qualities and goals. Realness welcomes us to scrutinize the accounts and assumptions forced upon us, engaging us to characterize ourselves.

Testing Presumptions and Convictions

Uncovering desires beyond societal expectations requires scrutinizing the suspicions and convictions that might have affected us. We should fundamentally inspect the stories we have incorporated and challenge their legitimacy. By doing so, we free ourselves up to the possibility of wants that stretch beyond cultural standards.

It is fundamental to ask ourselves intriguing inquiries:

"Whose desires am I truly pursuing?"

"What societal expectations have influenced my desires?"

"Are my desires in alignment with my values and true self?"

By testing presumptions and convictions, we make space for wants that are uniquely our own. We open ourselves up to additional opportunities and rethink achievement and satisfaction based on our conditions.

5. Developing Mindfulness

Developing mindfulness is critical to revealing cravings beyond societal expectations. It includes profound reflection and a readiness to investigate our inner scene. By fostering sharp identity mindfulness, we can separate between wants that are verifiable and those that are driven by outer impacts.

Mindfulness permits us to perceive the unobtrusive signals and pokes from our instincts the calm murmurs of our true cravings. Through practices like contemplation, journaling, or participating in care, we can reinforce our association with our internal identities and gain clarity on our most profound longings.

6. Taking advantage of Inward Qualities and Interests

Uncovering desires beyond societal expectations includes taking advantage of our internal qualities and interests. Our qualities are the core values that characterize us, while our interests are the exercises that light our excitement and give us pleasure. Investigating these parts of ourselves assists us in revealing longings that line up with our most genuine selves.

Pondering our guiding principle empowers us to distinguish wants that are in line with what we hold dear. Whether it is credibility, sympathy, imagination, or opportunity, our cravings frequently spring from the well of our qualities. Essentially, investigating our interests and taking part in exercises that charm our consideration gives us significant experiences into our most profound longings.

7. Embracing Individuality and Uniqueness

Uncovering desires beyond societal expectations requires embracing our individuality and uniqueness. Every one of us is brought into the world with a particular arrangement of characteristics, gifts, and goals that should be respected. By embracing our uniqueness, we oppose the strain to adjust and praise the variety of wants that exist within mankind.

It is essential to recall that there is no one-size-fits-all way to deal with wants. Every individual's process is exceptional, and our longings mirror the complexities of our own encounters, inclinations, and dreams. By embracing our individuality, we create a world that embraces the limitlessness of human longings and commends the extravagance of our aggregate embroidery.

8. Overcoming Fear and Judgment

Uncovering desires beyond societal expectations frequently includes beating dread and anxiety toward judgment. Society might label specific longings as flighty or ridiculous, prompting self-uncertainty and aversion to chasing after them. Nonetheless, it is vital to perceive that our cravings are substantial, paying little mind to how they might be seen by others.

To beat dread and judgment, we should develop self-acknowledgment and self-conviction. We should confide in our own instincts and honor the cravings that reverberate profoundly inside us. Encircling ourselves with a strong local area and looking for motivation from people who have sought after their valid longings can give us the consolation and solidarity to beat outer tensions.

9. Embracing a Fulfilling Life

By recognizing and seeking after our certified longings, we recover our independence and live in harmony with our most genuine selves. We live a daily existence that is legitimate, significant, and profoundly fulfilling.

Embracing desires beyond cultural assumptions empowers us to reclassify achievement and satisfaction according to our very own preferences. We shift the concentration from outer approval to inner fulfillment. Our longings become the compass that guides us towards an existence of direction, satisfaction, and self-realization.

All in all, revealing cravings past cultural assumptions is a freeing and extraordinary cycle. It includes embracing validness, testing suspicions, developing mindfulness, and embracing our independence. By uncovering our valid longings, we recover our independence, create a daily existence that mirrors our most genuine selves, and contribute to a world that commends the variety of human goals. Embracing past cultural assumptions permits us to carry on with a day-to-day existence that is interestingly our own a day-to-day existence that is profoundly satisfying and consistent with what our identity is.

Aligning Your Desires with Your True Self

Aligning your desires with your true self is a transformative and empowering process that brings forth a life of authenticity, fulfillment, and purpose. It involves connecting with the essence of who you are, understanding your values and passions, and consciously directing your actions towards desires that resonate with your deepest longings. Together, we will explore the significance of aligning your desires with your true self and discover the steps to embark on this transformative journey.

1. Embracing Self-Discovery

Aligning your desires with your true self begins with embracing self-discovery. It is an invitation to delve deep into your inner world and uncover the essence of who you are. Self-discovery involves exploring your thoughts, feelings, beliefs, values, and experiences with curiosity and openness.

Through self-discovery practices like journaling, meditation, and introspection, you gain valuable insights into your true desires. You connect with your inner wisdom, intuition, and authentic voice. Self-discovery allows you to distinguish between desires that are influenced by external factors and those that arise from the depths of your being.

2. Identifying Core Values

Aligning your desires with your true self requires a clear understanding of your core values. Core values are the guiding principles that define what is most important to you. They reflect your authentic self and act as a compass for making decisions and setting intentions.

By reflecting on and identifying your core values, you gain clarity on the desires that align with them. For example, if one of your core values is creativity, your desires may revolve around expressing yourself through artistic endeavors. When you align your desires with your core values, you create a life that reflects your truest self and brings you a deep sense of fulfillment.

3. Cultivating Self-Awareness

Self-awareness is a fundamental aspect of aligning your desires with your true self. It involves becoming conscious of your thoughts, emotions, and patterns of behavior. Through self-awareness, you gain a deeper understanding of how your desires align with your authentic self.

Practices like mindfulness, meditation, and self-reflection foster self-awareness. They allow you to observe your desires without judgment and recognize the patterns and motivations behind them. Self-awareness helps you discern whether your desires stem from your true self or are influenced by external expectations.

4. Listening to Your Intuition

Aligning your desires with your true self requires listening to the whispers of your intuition. Intuition is your inner compass, a deep knowing that guides you towards what feels right and resonant.

Listening to your intuition involves creating space for stillness and silence. It requires trusting your inner voice and honoring the nudges and insights that arise within you. Your intuition often speaks softly, but its guidance can lead you towards desires that are in harmony with your authentic self.

5. Letting Go of External Expectations

Aligning your desires with your true self necessitates letting go of external expectations. Society, family, and cultural influences can shape your desires, leading you to pursue goals and aspirations that may not align with your truest self. By releasing the need for external validation, you free yourself to embrace desires that reflect your authentic longings.

Letting go of external expectations requires self-acceptance and self-compassion. It involves recognizing that your desires are unique and valid, even if they differ from societal norms. By releasing the grip of external expectations, you create space for your authentic desires to emerge and flourish.

6. Seeking Clarity Through Reflection

Aligning your desires with your true self involves seeking clarity through reflection. Take time to reflect on your desires, asking yourself thought-provoking questions:

"What brings me joy and fulfillment?"

"What activities make me lose track of time?"

"If I had no fear or limitations, what would I truly desire?"

Through reflection, you gain clarity on the desires that resonate deeply with your true self. Reflection allows you to discern whether your current desires are in alignment with your authentic longings or if there are adjustments to be made.

7. Embracing Courageous Action

Aligning your desires with your true self requires taking courageous action. Once you have identified your authentic desires, it is essential to take deliberate steps towards manifesting them in your life. This may involve stepping out of your comfort zone, overcoming fears, and embracing vulnerability.

Courageous action propels you forward on the path of aligning your desires with your true self. It may involve making changes in your career, relationships, or lifestyle. By taking inspired action, you align your thoughts, intentions, and behaviors with your authentic desires, creating a life that reflects your truest self.

8. Nurturing Self-Trust and Self-Compassion

Aligning your desires with your true self requires nurturing self-trust and self-compassion. Trust yourself to make choices that honor your authentic desires, even when they seem unconventional or go against societal expectations. Cultivate self-compassion as you navigate the journey, knowing that aligning your desires with your true self is a process of growth and self-discovery.

Nurturing self-trust and self-compassion involves celebrating your progress, acknowledging your strengths, and embracing imperfections. It is about honoring your own unique journey and giving yourself permission to evolve and redefine your desires along the way.

9. Embracing a Life of Authenticity and Fulfillment

Aligning your desires with your true self leads to a life of authenticity and fulfillment. By embracing your authentic desires, you create a sense of harmony and alignment between your inner world and your outer experiences. You live a life that reflects your truest self, bringing you a deep sense of joy, purpose, and meaning.

By embracing a life of authenticity and fulfillment, you inspire others to do the same. Your aligned desires become a beacon of inspiration, encouraging others to connect with their true selves and pursue their own authentic desires. As you align your desires with your true self, you contribute to a world where individuals are empowered to live authentically and create lives of fulfillment and purpose.

Chapter 3

Putting forth Clear and Convincing Objectives

Objectives are the guides that guide us towards our ideal results. They give us direction, reason, and inspiration to pursue our fantasies and goals. Laying out clear and convincing objectives is fundamental for making progress and achieving satisfaction in different parts of our lives. Let's see the significance of putting forth clear and convincing objectives and find successful procedures to characterize and seek after them.

1. The Force of Clear and Convincing Objectives

Clear and convincing objectives act as reference points that enlighten our ideal objections. They give us clarity and concentration, assisting us with directing our energy, time, and assets towards significant results. Clear objectives empower us to quantify progress, track accomplishments, and pursue informed choices en route.

Convincing objectives fuel our inspiration and assurance. They motivate us to get out of our usual ranges of familiarity, beat deterrents, and continue even with difficulties. At the point when our objectives line up with our interests, values, and legitimate cravings, they become strong drivers of self-improvement and change.

2. Thinking about Your Cravings and Yearnings

Defining clear and convincing objectives starts with considering your cravings and goals. Carve out the opportunity to investigate what's most important to you and what you need to accomplish in various aspects of your life profession, connections, self-awareness, wellbeing—and that's just the beginning.

Thinking about your longings includes contemplation and mindfulness. Ask yourself intriguing inquiries:

"What gives me pleasure and satisfaction?"

"What is it that I need to achieve for the time being and for the long haul?"

"How would I imagine my optimal future?"

By digging deeply into your cravings and yearnings, you gain clarity on the objectives that really resonate with your valid self.

3. Making Objectives Shrewd

To guarantee lucidity and adequacy, it is vital to make your objectives Savvy: Explicit, Quantifiable, Feasible, Applicable, and Time-bound.

Specific: Clearly characterize your objectives, staying away from unclear or questionable proclamations. Be exact about what you need to accomplish and verbalize your expectations with clarity.

Measurable: Lay out substantial standards to quantify your advancement and achievement. Characterize explicit measurements, like achievements, cutoff times, or quantitative markers, to check your progress.

Achievable: Put forth objectives that are inside your compass and line up with your abilities, assets, and conditions. While it is essential to challenge yourself, guarantee that your objectives are reasonable and achievable.

Relevant: Adjust your objectives to your general vision, values, and long-term yearnings. Guarantee that your objectives are significant and applicable to your own proficient development.

Time-bound: Set explicit timetables or cutoff times for accomplishing your objectives. Laying out the need to get a move on assists you with keeping on track, inspired, and responsible.

Making objectives Savvy behavior improves the probability of progress and gives an unmistakable guide to activity.

4. Separating Objectives into Significant Stages

Whenever you have characterized your unmistakable and convincing objectives, separate them into noteworthy stages. Stalling objectives into reasonable errands dodges overpower and gives a guide to advance. It permits you to zero in on unambiguous activities and measure your progress en route.

Begin by recognizing the significant achievements or key activities expected to accomplish your objectives. Then, at that point, separate them further into more modest, noteworthy stages. Dole out cutoff times or courses of events for each step, making an organized game plan.

By separating your objectives into significant stages, you transform them from unique dreams into unmistakable and attainable targets.

5. Fostering an Activity Plan

To successfully pursue your objectives, foster a thorough activity plan. An activity plan frames the particular systems, assignments, and assets expected to accomplish your objectives. It gives a guide to progress and guarantees that you stay coordinated and centered in the meantime.

While fostering an activity plan, think about the accompanying components:

Distinguish explicit errands or activities expected to accomplish every achievement or step.

Decide the assets, abilities, and backing expected to achieve each assignment.

Lay out a timetable for getting done with every responsibility and arriving at achievements.

Expect possible obstructions or difficulties and foster alternate courses of action.

Routinely audit and update your activity plan on a case-by-case basis.

A very well-planned activity plan fills in as an outline for progress and keeps you on target towards your objectives.

6. Developing Responsibility and Following Advancement

Responsibility and progress are significant parts of objective accomplishment. By developing responsibility, you increase your responsibility and inspiration to completely finish your objectives. Following advancement permits you to quantify your progression, commend achievements, and make changes as needed.

There are a few methodologies to develop responsibility and track progress:

Share your objectives with a trusted companion, guide, or accountability accomplice who can offer help and consider you responsible.

Make a framework for keeping tabs on your development, for example, an objective diary, a task board application, or a visual following instrument.

Routinely survey and evaluate your progress against your activity plan, making changes or refinements on a case-by-case basis.

Celebrate little triumphs en route to keeping up with inspiration and force.

By supporting responsibility and following advancement, you keep up with concentration and energy towards your objectives.

7. Embracing Versatility and Adaptability

While putting forth clear objectives is fundamental, embracing versatility and flexibility is likewise significant. Perceive that life is dynamic and that conditions might change along your excursion. Be open to changing your objectives and activity plans on a case-by-case basis to remain aligned with your developing desires and needs.

Embracing flexibility permits you to explore startling difficulties, take advantage of new chances, and refine your objectives in view of newly discovered bits of knowledge and encounters. It is an update to say that the course of objective pursuit is pretty much as significant as the actual objective.

8. Developing a Development Mentality

Developing a development mentality is fundamental for laying out clear and convincing objectives. A development mentality is the conviction that capacities and insight can be created through devotion and exertion. By taking on a development mentality, you approach difficulties with versatility, view disappointments as learning opportunities, and stay open to constant development and improvement.

To develop a development outlook:

Embrace difficulties as open doors for development and learning.

Reexamine disappointments as stepping stones towards progress.

Look for input and useful analysis to improve your abilities and execution.

Develop an energy for deep-rooted learning and self-awareness.

A growth mindset empowers you to set ambitious goals, persevere through obstacles, and embrace the journey of self-improvement.

Setting clear and compelling goals is a powerful catalyst for personal and professional growth. By reflecting on your desires, making goals SMART, breaking them down into actionable steps, and developing a comprehensive action plan, you create a roadmap for success. Cultivating accountability, tracking progress, embracing adaptability, and cultivating a growth mindset further propel you towards achieving your goals. Through the process of setting and pursuing clear and compelling goals, you realize your potential, unleash your inner capabilities, and create a life of fulfillment and purpose.

Defining Significant Objectives: The Way to Show Desires

Defining significant objectives is an extraordinary cycle that engages us to show our cravings and create an existence of direction, satisfaction and achievement. Significant objectives line up with our most profound goals, values, and interests, touching off our inspiration and impelling us towards the acknowledgment of our fantasies. Let's look at the significance of laying out significant objectives and find successful methodologies to characterize and seek after them.

1. The Meaning of Significant Objectives

Significant objectives give us an internal compass and inspiration. They go past shallow longings and tap into the pith of what our identity is. Significant objectives resonate with our valid selves, mirroring our qualities, interests, and longings. They fuel our inspiration and drive, moving us to conquer deterrents, embrace difficulties, and endure chasing after our fantasies.

At the point when we put forth significant objectives, we make a guide for showing our longings. These objectives become the guiding light that leads us towards self-improvement, self-completion, and a day-to-day existence that lines up with our most genuine selves. Significant objectives enable us to make a legacy and have a beneficial outcome for the world.

2. Considering Your Interests and Values

Putting forth significant objectives starts with profound reflection on your interests and values. Interests are the exercises, interests, or causes that touch off your energy and give you pleasure. Values are the core values that characterize what means a lot to you.

Ponder the accompanying inquiries to uncover your interests and values:

What exercises cause you to feel invigorated and satisfied?

What causes or issues do you often think deeply about?

What center standards guide your choices and activities?

By interfacing with your interests and values, you gain bits of knowledge about what is important to you. This self-reflection lays the groundwork for defining significant objectives that line up with your bona fide wants.

3. Adjusting Objectives for Your Life Vision

Significant objectives are in accordance with your life vision, the vision you hold for your optimal future. Your life vision envelops all parts of your life, including your profession, connections, self-awareness, and wellbeing, and that's just the beginning. It addresses the great embroidered artwork of the existence you imagine for yourself.

While laying out objectives, ensure they are aligned with your life vision. Ask yourself:

How do these objectives add to my general life vision?

Do these objectives line up with my fundamental beliefs and interests?

Will accomplishing these objectives bring me closer to the existence I want?

By adjusting your objectives to your life vision, you create an agreeable and coordinated way to deal with objective setting, moving you towards an existence of satisfaction and credibility.

4. Making Objectives Significant and Motivating

Significant objectives bring out a feeling of direction and motivation. They resound with your most profound cravings, inspiring fervor, excitement, and a significant feeling of satisfaction. At the point when your objectives hold individual importance, they become strong inspirations that fuel your assurance and responsibility.

To make your objectives significant and motivating, think about the accompanying viewpoints:

Association with your qualities: Guarantee that your objectives align with your fundamental beliefs. At the point when your objectives reflect the main thing to you, they become mixed with profound importance and reason.

Close-to-home reverberation: Think about how accomplishing these objectives will cause you to feel. Embrace objectives that inspire positive feelings like delight, satisfaction, and fervor.

Commitment and effect: Consider how your objectives add to an option that could be more significant than yourself. Objectives that decidedly affect others or society can improve their importance.

By implanting your objectives with importance and motivation, you develop a profound sense of direction that drives you forward during testing times.

5. Putting forth Sensible and Feasible Objectives

While significant objectives might rouse us to think ambitiously, putting forth reasonable and achievable goals is significant. Unreasonable objectives can prompt disappointment, demoralization, and a feeling of disappointment. While laying out objectives, think about your ongoing conditions, assets, and abilities.

Guarantee that your objectives are sensible by:

Surveying your ongoing abilities, information, and assets.

Separating bigger objectives into more modest, reasonable advances

Setting attainable achievements en route

Looking for help and direction when it's important.

By laying out reasonable and feasible objectives, you put yourself in a good position and keep a positive mentality all through your excursion.

6. Making a Strategy

A strategy is fundamental for achieving significant objectives. It gives a guide that frames the particular advances, methodologies, and assets expected to accomplish your ideal results. Making a game plan upgrades your concentration, association, and responsibility.

While making a strategy,

Separate your objectives into more modest, noteworthy undertakings.

Set cutoff times or timetables for each assignment or achievement.

Recognize the assets, abilities, and backing required.

Expect possible obstructions and foster emergency courses of action.

A very well-planned strategy fills in as a guidepost, assisting you with staying focused and making reliable headway towards your significant objectives.

7. Developing Diligence and Strength

Having significant objectives requires diligence and strength. Difficulties and mishaps are unavoidable on the way to progress. Developing a mentality of industriousness and strength guarantees that you can conquer hindrances, gain from disappointments, and drive forward towards your objectives.

To develop constancy and versatility:

Embrace a development outlook: View difficulties as open doors for development and learning.

Gain from disappointments: Separate examples from difficulties and use them to refine your methodology.

Look for help and inspiration. Encircle yourself with a strong organization that elevates and energizes you.

Celebrate little triumphs. Recognize and celebrate achievements en route to remaining persuaded.

By sustaining diligence and flexibility, you stay focused on your significant objectives and remain unflinching in their interests.

8. Routinely Checking on and Changing Objectives

Routinely exploring and changing your objectives is a vital part of the objective-setting process. As you progress on your excursion and gain new experiences, assessing the arrangement and pertinence of your goals is fundamental.

Intermittently audit your objectives by:

Surveying your advancement and estimating your accomplishments.

Considering whether your objectives actually resonate with your credible cravings and values

Changing or refining your objectives in light of new data or changes in your conditions

By exploring and changing your objectives, you guarantee that they stay significant and in accord with your developing yearnings.

9. Developing Appreciation and Observing Achievements

All through your objective-setting venture, develop appreciation and celebrate achievements en route. Appreciation moves your concentration to the current second, assisting you in valuing the progress you have made. Commending achievements gives you pride, helps inspire you, and builds up your obligation to your significant objectives.

Express gratitude by:

Considering the headway you have made

Celebrating little triumphs and achievements.

Perceiving the examples and development experienced en route

By developing appreciation and commending achievements, you inject your excursion with inspiration, satisfaction, and a feeling of achievement.

Laying out significant objectives is an extraordinary cycle that enables us to show our cravings and create an existence of direction, satisfaction, and achievement. By pondering our interests and values, adjusting objectives to our life vision, and making objectives significant and moving, we ignite our inspiration and drive. Defining practical and feasible objectives, making a strategy, and developing tirelessness and versatility impel us towards progress. Consistently exploring and changing objectives, developing appreciation, and commending achievements keeps us drawn in and roused. By putting forth significant objectives, we embark on an extraordinary excursion of self-revelation, self-awareness, and the indication of our true longings.

Creating S.M.A.R.T. Objectives: Explicit, Quantifiable, Reachable, Pertinent, Time-Bound

Laying out objectives is a fundamental piece of individual and expert development. In any case, to build the opportunities to effectively accomplish those objectives, it is vital to do so in a manner that guarantees clarity, concentration, and responsibility. S.M.A.R.T. objectives give a system for laying out objectives that are Explicit, Quantifiable, Feasible, Significant, and Time-Bound. In this section, we will investigate the meaning of creating S.M.A.R.T. objectives and figure out how to really apply this structure.

1. The Force of S.M.A.R.T. Objectives

S.M.A.R.T. objectives give an organized way to deal with objective setting, empowering people to set clear targets and characterize the way to accomplish them. By integrating the five critical components of Explicit, Quantifiable, Attainable, relevant, and Time-Bound, S.M.A.R.T. objectives improve concentration, inspiration, and responsibility.

Creating S.M.A.R.T. objectives engages people to:

Characterize explicit goals: S.M.A.R.T. objectives assist people with articulating definitively what they need to accomplish.

Measure progress and achievement: By consolidating quantifiable components, people can follow their progress and assess their accomplishments.

Keep up with inspiration and responsibility. Laying out attainable objectives that line up with individual capacities and goals guarantees support, inspiration, and responsibility.

Lay out pertinence and reason: S.M.A.R.T. objectives guarantee that people set goals that are significant and aligned with their general vision and values.

Execute powerfully while using time effectively: The time-bound part of S.M.A.R.T. objectives advances proficient preparation and prioritization.

2. Laying out Unambiguous Objectives

Explicit objectives are plainly characterized and rule out equivocalness or disarray. They answer the questions of what, why, who, and where. While putting forth unambiguous objectives, it is vital to be exact about what you need to accomplish and give subtleties that convey clarity to your targets.

To make your objectives explicit:

Obviously, state what you need to achieve.

Incorporate subtleties like explicit activities, targets, or results.

Indicate the reasons and inspirations driving your objectives.

Recognize the people or groups engaged in accomplishing the objectives.

Decide the area or setting where the objectives will be sought.

By defining explicit objectives, you give an unmistakable heading to your endeavors and upgrade your capacity to zero in on the ideal results.

3. Guaranteeing Quantifiable Objectives

Quantifiable objectives permit people to keep tabs on their development, survey their accomplishments, and remain responsible. Quantifiable objectives give substantial proof of accomplishment and act as designated stops along the way. By integrating measurements or rules for estimation, people can impartially assess their progress towards their objectives.

To guarantee your objectives are quantifiable,

Distinguish explicit measurements or markers to check progress.

Decide how you will gauge or measure your prosperity.

Separate bigger objectives into more modest achievements for simpler estimation.

Set explicit targets or benchmarks to hold nothing back.

By making your objectives quantifiable, you create a sense of responsibility and keep up with inspiration through the capacity to keep tabs on your development.

4. Laying out Reachable Objectives

Attainable objectives are inside your compass and line up with your abilities, assets, and conditions. It is critical to lay out objectives that stretch your capacities and motivate development, yet they ought to likewise be sensible and achievable. Laying out unreachable objectives can prompt dissatisfaction and demotivation.

To lay out reachable objectives:

Survey your ongoing abilities, assets, and constraints.

Separate bigger objectives into more modest, sensible undertakings.

Think about likely provocations or snags and foster procedures to conquer them.

Look for input or counsel from tutors or specialists to assess the attainability of your objectives.

By putting forth reachable objectives, you create a feeling of certainty and gather speed towards progress.

5. Guaranteeing Important Objectives

Important objectives are aligned with your general vision, values, and desires. They are significant and deliberate, reverberating with your own or proficient development. Defining pertinent objectives guarantees that your endeavors are guided towards goals that genuinely make a difference to you.

To guarantee your objectives are pertinent:

Adjust your objectives to your drawn-out vision or desired results.

Evaluate whether your objectives line up with your qualities, interests, or areas of interest.

Assess the effect and meaning of your objectives in relation to your general goals.

By defining important objectives, you create a feeling of direction and satisfaction, driving your responsibility and commitment.

6. Defining Time-Bound Objectives

Time-bound objectives have a characterized course of events or cutoff time for culmination. By laying out time imperatives, people feel the need to get a move on and focus on their endeavors successfully. Time-bound objectives assist with forestalling stalling and support productive use of time.

To lay out time-bound objectives:

Lay out unambiguous cutoff times or deadlines for every objective.

Separate your objectives into more modest, time-bound achievements or errands.

Consider the time expected for planning, execution, and assessment.

Screen your advancement routinely to guarantee you are on target within the allocated time span.

By defining time-bound objectives, you create a feeling of concentration, earnestness, and discipline, empowering you to make effective headway towards your ideal results.

7. Applying the S.M.A.R.T. System

To actually make S.M.A.R.T. objectives, incorporating every one of the five elements is fundamental: Explicit, Quantifiable, Feasible, Pertinent, and Time-Bound. The S.M.A.R.T. system gives an extensive way to deal with objective setting that boosts lucidity, concentration, and responsibility.

To apply the S.M.A.R.T. structure:

Begin by laying out unambiguous objectives that clearly characterize what you need to accomplish.

Guarantee your objectives are quantifiable by distinguishing standards or measurements for advancement and achievement.

Put forth attainable objectives that align with your abilities and assets.

Assess the significance of your objectives by evaluating their arrangement with your vision, values, and desires.

Lay out a period-headed viewpoint for every objective, integrating cutoff times or deadlines.

By integrating the S.M.A.R.T. structure into your objective-setting process, you make a strong starting point for progress and increment your possibilities of achieving your ideal results.

8. Evaluating and Updating Objectives

As you progress on your objective-setting venture, it is pivotal to audit and modify your objectives consistently. Conditions might change, new open doors might emerge, or needs might shift. By intermittently looking into and reexamining your objectives, you guarantee that they stay aligned with your developing desires.

To actually survey and reconsider your objectives,

Survey your advancement and assess whether your objectives are as yet important and significant.

Consider any outer variables or inside changes that might influence your objectives.

Adjust or refine your objectives to line up with your ongoing vision, values, and conditions.

Look for input from trusted tutors or counselors to acquire new viewpoints on your objectives.

By surveying and overhauling your objectives, you adjust to the powerful idea of life and make space for continued development and improvement.

Creating S.M.A.R.T. objectives is a strong way to deal with objective setting that improves clarity, concentration and responsibility. By putting forth objectives that are Explicit, Quantifiable, Feasible, Applicable, and Time-Bound, people increase their opportunities to effectively accomplish their ideal results. S.M.A.R.T. objectives provide an organized system that engages people to characterize goals, measure progress, remain spurred, lay out pertinence, and oversee time successfully. By integrating the S.M.A.R.T. structure into their objective-setting process, people make a strong starting point for progress and prepare for individual and expert development.

Setting Intentions: Harnessing the Power of Purposeful Goal Setting

Setting intentions is a transformative process that empowers individuals to align their thoughts, emotions, and actions towards purposeful goal setting. Intentions serve as the guiding principles that shape our goals, choices, and behaviors, leading us towards a life of fulfillment, authenticity, and success. In this chapter, we will explore the significance of setting intentions and learn how to harness their power in the process of goal setting.

1. Understanding the Power of Intentions

Intentions are the driving force behind our goals and aspirations. They go beyond the mere desire for specific outcomes and delve into the deeper realms of purpose, meaning, and authenticity. Intentions provide the foundation upon which we build our goals, influencing our thoughts, emotions, and actions.

Setting intentions is powerful because it:

creates clarity and focus: Intentions help us clarify our values, passions, and desires, allowing us to set goals that align with our truest selves.

Guides decision-making: Intentions act as a compass, guiding us in making choices that are in alignment with our values and long-term aspirations.

Enhances motivation and commitment: By setting intentions, we tap into our intrinsic motivation and develop a deep sense of purpose, fueling our commitment and perseverance.

cultivates mindfulness and presence: Intentions anchor us in the present moment, fostering mindfulness and awareness of our actions and their impact.

Shape our reality: Intentions have the power to shape our reality by influencing our beliefs, attitudes, and actions, ultimately leading us towards the realization of our goals.

2. Connecting with Your Inner Essence

Setting intentions begins with connecting with your inner essence—the core of who you are. It involves introspection, self-reflection, and cultivating a deep understanding of your values, passions, and authentic desires.

To connect with your inner essence:

Create space for quiet reflection and self-inquiry.

Tune in to your emotions, thoughts, and sensations.

Explore your values, passions, and deepest longings.

Identify the aspects of your life that bring you joy, fulfillment, and a sense of purpose.

By connecting with your inner essence, you gain valuable insights that inform your intentions and guide your goal-setting process.

3. Cultivating Clarity and Alignment

Setting intentions requires clarity and alignment between your inner desires and your external goals. It involves defining what truly matters to you and ensuring that your goals are in harmony with your values, passions, and long-term vision.

To cultivate clarity and alignment:

Reflect on your values, passions, and authentic desires.

Identify the areas of your life where you seek growth, improvement, or transformation.

Explore the ways in which your goals can contribute to your personal and professional development.

Assess whether your goals align with your core values and long-term aspirations.

By cultivating clarity and alignment, you set the stage for purposeful goal-setting and a life that reflects your truest self.

4. Setting Positive and empowered Intentions

Intentions should be positive, empowering, and aligned with your desired outcomes. They should reflect your aspirations, growth mindset, and belief in your own abilities to achieve success.

When setting intentions:

Phrase them in positive and affirmative language.

Focus on what you want to create or experience rather than what you want to avoid.

Embrace empowering beliefs and affirmations that support your intentions.

Align your intentions with your long-term vision and the impact you want to make in the world.

By setting positive and empowering intentions, you cultivate a mindset that fosters growth, resilience, and success.

5. Creating Rituals and Practices

To solidify your intentions and integrate them into your daily life, create rituals and practices that reinforce their importance. Rituals provide a dedicated space and time for connecting with your intentions, amplifying their impact and significance.

Consider incorporating the following practices into your routine:

Journaling: Write down your intentions, reflect on their meaning, and track your progress.

Visualization: Imagine yourself embodying your intentions and experiencing the emotions associated with their realization.

Meditation: Practice mindfulness or guided meditation to center yourself and connect with your intentions.

Affirmations: Repeat affirmations that reinforce your intentions, beliefs, and commitment to your goals.

Gratitude: Express gratitude for the progress you have made towards your intentions and the opportunities that lie ahead.

By integrating rituals and practices, you anchor your intentions in your daily life, deepening your connection and commitment to their manifestation.

6. Embracing Flexibility and Adaptability

While setting intentions is a powerful practice, it is important to embrace flexibility and adaptability. Life is dynamic, and circumstances may change along your journey. Embracing flexibility allows you to adjust your intentions and goals as needed, ensuring they remain aligned with your evolving aspirations.

To embrace flexibility and adaptability:

Regularly reassess your intentions in light of new insights or changes in your circumstances.

Be open to alternative paths or opportunities that may arise along the way.

Embrace the lessons and growth that come from unexpected twists and turns.

Practice self-compassion and let go of attachments to specific outcomes.

By embracing flexibility and adaptability, you remain open to the flow of life and allow your intentions to evolve in alignment with your highest potential.

7. Aligning Actions with Intentions

Setting intentions is not enough; it is essential to align your actions with your intentions. Intentions without action remain mere aspirations. By taking deliberate steps towards your goals, you bridge the gap between your intentions and their realization.

To align your actions with your intentions:

Break down your intentions into actionable steps.

Create a plan of action that outlines the specific tasks and milestones to be achieved.

Prioritize and allocate time for activities that support your intentions.

Stay focused and committed to taking consistent action towards your goals.

Regularly evaluate your progress and make adjustments as necessary.

By aligning your actions with your intentions, you embody the transformation you seek and bring your goals to fruition.

8. Embracing Mindfulness and Gratitude

Mindfulness and gratitude are powerful practices that enhance the manifestation of your intentions. Mindfulness cultivates presence, allowing you to fully engage with the present moment and align your actions with your intentions. Gratitude opens your heart to appreciation, amplifying positive emotions and attracting more of what you desire.

To embrace mindfulness and gratitude:

Practice mindfulness meditation to cultivate presence and awareness.

Incorporate gratitude practices, such as a gratitude journal or daily gratitude reflection.

Notice the progress you have made towards your intentions and celebrate small victories along the way.

Express gratitude for the opportunities, resources, and support that contribute to the manifestation of your intentions.

By embracing mindfulness and gratitude, you deepen your connection with your intentions, amplify positive energy, and attract more opportunities for their realization.

Setting intentions is a transformative process that harnesses the power of purposeful goal-setting. Intentions provide the guiding principles that shape our goals, choices, and behaviors. By connecting with our inner essence, cultivating clarity and alignment, and setting positive and empowering intentions, we pave the way for a life of fulfillment and success. Through rituals and practices, flexibility and adaptability, aligning actions with intentions, and embracing mindfulness and gratitude, we bridge the gap between our intentions and their manifestation. By setting intentions, we tap into our deepest aspirations, align with our truest selves, and create a life that reflects our authentic desires.

Chapter 4

Conquering restrictive Convictions and Fears

Restricting convictions and fears are inside boundaries that can impede self-awareness, ruin progress, and keep people from accomplishing their maximum capacity. They are the willful restrictions that keep us from chasing after our fantasies and goals. Conquering these restricting convictions and fears is an extraordinary cycle that enables people to break free from their imperatives and open their actual potential. In this part, we will investigate the meaning of beating restrictive convictions and fears and learn viable methodologies to overcome them.

1. Figuring out Restricting Convictions and Fears

Restricting convictions are profoundly imbued thought examples or convictions that compel our reasoning, conduct, and potential. They frequently come from previous encounters, cultural molding, or negative self-talk. Normal instances of restricting convictions include "I'm not adequate," "I don't merit achievement," or "I'm too old to even think about beginning."

Fears, then again, are personal reactions to perceived dangers or risks. They can appear as dread of disappointment, anxiety toward judgment, apprehension about vulnerability, or anxiety toward dismissal. Fears are established in our instinctual survival reaction and are often nonsensical or lopsided compared to the genuine dangers implied.

Both restricting convictions and fears create a mental boundary that keeps people from seeking after their objectives, facing challenges, and embracing their actual potential.

2. Perceiving Restricting Convictions and Fears

The most vital phase in conquering restrictive convictions and fears is to perceive and recognize their reality. Commonly, these convictions and fears work in our psyche, impacting our considerations and ways of behaving without our cognizant mindfulness.

To perceive restrictive convictions and fears:

Practice self-reflection and thoughtfulness.

Focus on your self-talk and the stories you tell yourself.

Notice your profound reactions and examples of conduct in different circumstances.

Search for repeating topics or examples of self-questioning, self-analysis, or evasion.

By becoming mindful of your restrictive convictions and fears, you can start to challenge and conquer them.

3. Testing and Restricting Convictions

Testing and restricting convictions is a course of scrutinizing their legitimacy, rethinking negative considerations, and supplanting them with engaging and steady convictions. It includes testing the proof behind your restricting convictions, inspecting elective points of view, and assembling proof that goes against these convictions.

To challenge restrictive convictions:

Recognize the particular restrictive conviction that is keeping you down.

Question the proof supporting that conviction. Ask yourself, "Is this conviction in light of realities or suppositions?"

Search for counterexamples or proof that goes against the conviction.

Reexamine the restricting conviction into a positive, engaging assertion.

Practice confirmations or positive self-talk that builds up your new conviction.

By testing and rethinking restricting convictions, you start to shift your mentality and free yourself up to additional opportunities and potential open doors.

4. Going up against Fears

Going up against fears includes confronting them head-on and finding proactive ways to conquer them. It requires boldness, flexibility, and an eagerness to step beyond your usual range of familiarity. Evasion just sustains dread, while standing up to fears assists you in building certainty and versatility.

To defy fears:

Distinguish the particular apprehension that is keeping you down.

Investigate the main driver of trepidation and its fundamental triggers.

Separate the trepidation into more modest, sensible advances.

Slowly open yourself to the trepidation in a controlled and safe way.

Look for help from companions, tutors, or specialists who can give direction and support.

By going up against your feelings of trepidation, you progressively lessen their power and gain trust in your capacity to conquer them.

5. Developing Self-Empathy and Self-Conviction

Developing self-empathy and self-conviction is fundamental during the time spent beating restrictive convictions and fears. Self-sympathy includes treating yourself with generosity, understanding, and acknowledgment, particularly when confronting difficulties or mishaps. Self-conviction is confidence in your own capacities, value, and potential for progress.

To develop self-empathy and self-conviction:

Practice taking care of oneself and focusing on your prosperity.

Offer yourself thoughtfulness and understanding while confronting misfortunes or difficulties.

Praise your assets, accomplishments, and progress.

Encircle yourself with positive impacts and strong connections.

Challenge negative self-talk and supplant it with positive insistence.

By developing self-empathy and self-conviction, you construct versatility and fortify your internal establishment to beat restricting convictions and fears.

6. Making a move and Embracing Development

Making a move is an urgent move toward defeating restrictive convictions and fears. Activity assists with testing and invalidating restricting convictions, while likewise gathering certainty and making speed towards your objectives. Embracing development includes venturing beyond your usual range of familiarity and embracing open doors for learning, investigation, and self-awareness.

To make a move and embrace development:

Separate your objectives into little, reachable advances.

Set practical and feasible achievements to keep tabs on your development.

Challenge yourself to step beyond your usual range of familiarity.

Embrace the amazing doors that open for learning and self-awareness.

Praise your triumphs, regardless of how little.

By making a move and embracing development, you create a positive input circle that supports your capacity to overcome restricting convictions and fears.

7. Looking for Help and Responsibility

Looking for help and responsibility from others can be extraordinarily effective in defeating restrictive convictions and fears. Confident companions, tutors, or mentors can give direction, consolation, and an outside viewpoint that assists you in exploring difficulties and remaining spurred.

To look for help and responsibility:

Share your objectives, difficulties, and fears with trusted people.

Look for direction or mentorship from somebody who has overcome similar restrictive convictions or fears.

Join a steady local area or gathering that has comparable goals or battles.

Lay out normal registrations or responsibility meetings with a believed responsibility accomplice.

By looking for help and responsibility, you create an organization of consolation and help that reinforces your endeavors to overcome restricting convictions and fears.

8. Embracing a Development Outlook

Embracing a development outlook is fundamental during the time spent conquering restricting convictions and fears. A development outlook is the conviction that knowledge, capacities, and gifts can be created through exertion, practice, and learning. It supports flexibility, interest, and a readiness to embrace difficulties as open doors for development.

To embrace a development outlook:

Embrace difficulties and view them as open doors for learning and improvement.

Embrace disappointment as a stepping stone towards progress and learning.

Develop an oddity and yearn for information and self-awareness.

Look for input and useful analysis to upgrade your abilities and execution.

Cultivate confidence in your capacity to learn, adjust, and develop.

By embracing a development mentality, you change deterrents into open doors, defeat restricting convictions, and vanquish your feelings of dread.

All in all, beating restricting convictions and fears is an extraordinary excursion that engages people to break free from willful imperatives and open their actual potential. By perceiving and testing restricting convictions, facing fears, developing self-sympathy and self-conviction, making a move, looking for help, and embracing a development mentality, people can rise above their limits and accomplish their objectives. Through this cycle, people find their inward strength, flexibility, and capacity to create the existence they want. By beating restrictive convictions and fears, people free themselves up to a universe of potential outcomes, development, and satisfaction.

Identifying and Challenging Restrictive Beliefs

Restrictive beliefs are thought patterns that are deeply ingrained in our minds and prevent us from realizing our full potential. They are the purposeful boundaries that limit our reasoning, conduct, and activities. These beliefs frequently result from experiences in the past, social conditioning, or self-doubt. Recognizing and testing restricting convictions is an extraordinary interaction that engages people to break free from these requirements and open up additional opportunities for development, achievement, and satisfaction. In this part, we will investigate the meaning of recognizing and testing restrictive convictions and learn powerful systems to conquer them.

1. The Effect of Restricting Convictions

Restricting convictions can fundamentally affect different parts of our lives. They can have an impact on how we see ourselves, our relationships, and our professional development. These convictions go about as channels through which we decipher the world, impacting our considerations, feelings, and activities. They limit our true capacity, keep us away from facing challenges, and keep us from seeking after our fantasies and desires.

Restricting convictions can appear in different regions; for example,

Self-esteem and confidence: Accepting that we do not merit achievement or satisfaction

Skills and abilities: believing that we are insufficiently skilled or capable to accomplish our objectives

Relationships: Accepting that we are ashamed of affection, trust, or sound associations

Ample wealth and money: Accepting that we are bound to battle monetarily or that cash is intrinsically negative

Achievement and achievement: Accepting that achievement is held for other people and not feasible for ourselves

By recognizing and testing these restricting convictions, we can break free from their limitations and develop an outlook that enables us to seek after our objectives and dreams.

2. Perceiving Restricting Convictions

The most vital phase in beating restrictive convictions is to perceive and recognize their reality. Ordinarily, these convictions work in our psyche, affecting our contemplations and ways of behaving without our cognizant mindfulness. By bringing them into our cognizant mindfulness, we gain the ability to challenge and change them.

To perceive restrictive convictions:

Notice your self-talk and the stories you tell yourself.

Focus on repeating examples of negative considerations or self-questioning.

Take note of how you react emotionally to various circumstances.

Ponder the convictions you hold about yourself, others, and the world.

Analyze any regions of your day-to-day existence where you feel stuck or restricted.

By perceiving the presence of restricting convictions, you can start the process involved in revealing their fundamental causes and testing their legitimacy.

3. Uncovering the Hidden Causes

Restricting convictions frequently have fundamental causes that add to their arrangement. These causes can incorporate previous encounters, cultural molding, or the impact of critical individuals in our lives. Understanding the starting points of these convictions gives us significant insight into their inclination and assists us in tending to them all the more successfully.

To discover the root causes of restrictive beliefs:

Think about your previous encounters and huge occasions that might have impacted your convictions.

Think about how your beliefs are shaped by cultural or societal conditioning.

Identify authority figures or influential individuals whose beliefs may have influenced your own.

Examine any recurring ideas or messages that have affected how you see yourself.

By revealing the fundamental reasons for restricting convictions, you gain a more profound comprehension of how they were shaped and can start to challenge their legitimacy.

4. Testing the Legitimacy of Restricting Convictions

Testing the legitimacy of restricting convictions includes scrutinizing their exactness and inspecting the proof that supports or discredits them. It necessitates a willingness to question our preconceived notions and investigate other points of view.

To question limiting beliefs' veracity:

Determine the specific limiting belief that prevents you from moving forward.

Examine the supporting evidence for that belief. Ask yourself, "Is this conviction in light of realities or suspicions?"

Look for evidence or counterexamples that refute the belief.

Think about other beliefs or perspectives that might be more empowering and supportive.

To challenge the belief's validity, engage in critical thinking and logical reasoning.

By testing the legitimacy of restricting convictions, you make space for additional opportunities and pave the way for self-awareness and change.

Limiting Beliefs Can Be Reframed By Replacing them with More empowered and Supportive beliefs. It requires us to consciously select thoughts and beliefs that are in line with our goals and aspirations.

To reexamine restricting convictions:

Distinguish the particular restrictive conviction you need to reevaluate.

Counter the limitations of the original belief with a positive, empowering alternative belief.

Repeat the new belief to yourself frequently and write it down.

Look for examples and evidence to back up the new belief.

Practice confirmations or positive self-talk that supports the new conviction.

You gradually rewire your thinking patterns and replace limiting beliefs with empowering ones by consistently reinforcing the new belief through repetition and positive self-talk.

5. Looking for Elective Points of View and Backing

Looking for elective points of view and backing from others can be instrumental in testing and restricting convictions. Confident companions, guides, or mentors can offer new viewpoints, useful criticism, and consolation as you explore the most common way of conquering these convictions.

To look for elective viewpoints and backing,

Discuss your restrictive beliefs with trusted people.

Look for direction from tutors or mentors who can give experiences and systems for testing and rethinking restrictive convictions.

Encircle yourself with positive impacts and steady connections.

Participate in conversations or exercises that open you to alternate points of view and thoughts.

You will gain new insights, broaden your understanding, and bolster your efforts to challenge and overcome limiting beliefs if you look for support and alternative perspectives.

6. Making A motivated Move

Making a motivated move is a crucial stage in testing restrictive convictions. Activity assists with building proof and encounters that go against the impediments of these convictions, continuously disintegrating their hold over us. By venturing outside our usual range of familiarity and chasing after our objectives, we gain energy and strengthen our confidence in our own capacities.

To make an enlivened move:

Separate your objectives into little, reasonable advances.

Start by doing things that support your new beliefs.

Embrace open doors for development and learning.

Celebrate little triumphs en route to supporting a positive relationship by making a move.

By making a motivated move, you fabricate certainty, strength, and a feeling of strengthening, which continuously debilitates the hold of restricting convictions.

7. Embracing Self-Reflection and Persistent Development

Defeating restrictive convictions is a continuous cycle that requires self-reflection, thoughtfulness, and nonstop development. It is absolutely necessary to evaluate and challenge any new limiting beliefs on a regular basis as you move forward in your journey.

to accept self-reflection and continual development:

Put aside opportunities for reflection and self-reflection.

Ponder your convictions, considerations, and ways of behaving consistently.

Look for open doors for self-improvement, like perusing, going to studios, or taking part in rehearsals that cultivate mindfulness.

Embrace a development outlook and view difficulties as open doors for learning and development.

You can cultivate resilience, adaptability, and an empowered mindset by embracing self-reflection and continuous growth. These traits will help you overcome limiting beliefs over time.

All in all, recognizing and testing restricting convictions is a groundbreaking cycle that enables people to break free from deliberate limitations and open their actual potential. By perceiving and recognizing these convictions, uncovering their hidden causes, testing their legitimacy, and reexamining them with other options, people can create additional opportunities for development, achievement, and satisfaction. Looking for elective viewpoints and backing, making an enlivened move, and embracing self-reflection and constant development are fundamental parts of the excursion to defeat restricting convictions. People develop a mindset that enables them to pursue their objectives, recognize their true potential, and construct the life they desire by challenging and transforming these beliefs.

Developing a Positive Mentality for Progress

A positive mentality is an integral asset that can change our lives and push us towards progress. It includes developing a hopeful viewpoint, embracing a development outlook, and creating strength despite challenges. A positive outlook enables us to conquer obstructions, face challenges, and immediately jump on chances. In this section, we will investigate the meaning of developing a positive mentality for progress and learn reasonable systems to cultivate energy in our lives.

1. Figuring out the Force of a Positive Mentality

A positive outlook is a psychological mentality that focuses on potential outcomes, developments, and arrangements. An optimistic outlook sees mishaps as open doors for learning, sees difficulties as stepping stones to progress, and has confidence in our own capacities to accomplish our objectives. A positive outlook isn't tied in with preventing hardships or pessimistic feelings, but rather about deciding to move toward them with versatility, hopefulness, and confidence in our ability to defeat them.

The force of a positive mentality lies in its capacity to:

Boost resilience: A positive mentality empowers us to return quickly from misfortunes, gain from disappointments, and continue despite difficulties.

Boost development and learning: It cultivates a development outlook where we consider disappointments and errors to be potential open doors for development and improvement.

Inspiration and efficiency: A positive mentality fills our inspiration, motivates us to make a move, and builds our efficiency and concentration.

Work on, generally speaking, prosperity. By cultivating gratitude, optimism, and self-belief, it increases happiness, satisfaction, and overall well-being.

Draw in valuable open doors: A positive mentality creates a vigorous vibration that draws in certain potential open doors and encounters into our lives.

Moving Points of View: Embracing a Development Mentality

A development mentality is the conviction that our capacities and insights can be created through exertion, practice, and learning. It is the underpinning of a positive mentality as it urges us to embrace difficulties, continue notwithstanding misfortunes, and consider disappointments to be open doors for development.

To embrace a development outlook:

Perceive that capacities and abilities are not fixed attributes but instead characteristics that can be developed and worked on after some time.

Embrace difficulties as opening doors for learning and self-awareness.

Prioritize effort, tenacity, and a willingness to learn over quick wins.

Develop an oddity and want information, searching out new encounters and learning about potential open doors.

Reevaluate disappointments as significant input and stepping stones to progress.

By embracing a development mentality, we encourage an inspirational outlook that upholds our excursion towards progress.

2. Practicing Gratitude and Positivity

Practicing gratitude and positivity is a powerful way to cultivate a positive mindset. It involves consciously focusing on the positive aspects of our lives, appreciating what we have, and acknowledging the good in ourselves and others. Gratitude and positivity create a shift in our perception, allowing us to see the abundance and opportunities that surround us.

To put gratitude and positivity into practice:

Write down three things you are grateful for each day in a gratitude journal.

Practice care and enjoy the present moment, appreciating the basic delights throughout everyday life.

Encircle yourself with positive impacts, like elevating books, webcasts, or steady connections.

Rethink negative contemplations or circumstances by searching for the silver lining or examples learned.

Positive self-talk and affirmations can help you maintain a positive outlook.

By practicing appreciation and inspiration, we train our brains to zero in on the positive parts of our lives, cultivating a positive and hopeful standpoint.

3. Building Self-Belief and Confidence

A positive mindset is built on self-belief and confidence. At the point when we have confidence in our capacities, assets, and potential, we approach difficulties with identity confirmation and strength. Developing self-conviction and certainty requires recognizing our accomplishments, embracing our uniqueness, and reexamining self-questioning.

To cultivate self-belief and confidence:

Praise your accomplishments, regardless of how little, and recognize your assets and capacities.

Kindness and understanding toward yourself are examples of self-compassion.

Be surrounded by people who are upbeat, encouraging, and believe in your potential.

Positive affirmations can take the place of self-doubt and negative self-talk.

Get out of your usual range of familiarity and proceed with potentially dangerous courses of action, progressively extending your certainty and faith in yourself.

We develop the inner foundation necessary to accept challenges and pursue success with a positive mindset by cultivating self-belief and confidence.

4. Nurturing a Supportive Environment

Our current circumstances play a huge part in forming our mentality. To cultivate a supportive environment, we need to surround ourselves with positive influences, have relationships that are supportive of us, and have opportunities to learn and grow. It incorporates creating a space that cultivates inspiration, empowers self-improvement, and offers the help expected to pursue our objectives.

To cultivate a supportive atmosphere:

Be surrounded by positive, like-minded people who lift you up and inspire you.

Look for coaches or mentors who can guide you, encourage you, and hold you accountable.

Participate in exercises and leisure activities that line up with your interests and give you pleasure.

Make an actual space that advances unwinding, concentration, and inventiveness.

Constantly look for valuable open doors for self-improvement, like going to studios or getting networks of people together with comparative objectives.

By sustaining a strong climate, we make the ground ripe for developing a positive mentality and encouraging our own and proficient development.

5. Embracing Optimism and Resilience

Optimism and resilience are necessary components of a positive mentality. Expecting positive outcomes, looking for solutions, and maintaining a positive outlook are all components of optimism. Flexibility is the capacity to quickly recover from misfortunes, adjust to change, and endure even affliction.

To embrace resilience and optimism:

Reframe negative circumstances by focusing on potential solutions and growth opportunities.

Develop a positive inner discourse by testing negative contemplations and supplanting them with positive confirmations.

Develop a feeling of trust and conviction that difficulties are brief and can prompt development and additional opportunities.

Practice taking care of oneself and focusing on exercises that advance profound and mental prosperity.

Utilize setbacks and failures as stepping stones toward success.

By embracing confidence and versatility, we foster the strength and mentality necessary to explore difficulties and defeat impediments with an inspirational perspective. Beating

6. Self-Restricting Convictions

Self-restricting convictions are mental obstructions that keep us from seeking after our objectives and understanding our maximum capacity. Defeating these convictions is a significant step in developing a positive mentality. It involves challenging and refocusing the beliefs that keep us from growing and succeeding and replacing them with empowering beliefs.

To conquer self-restricting convictions:

Distinguish the particular self-restricting conviction that is keeping you down.

Inspect the proof that supports or invalidates the conviction.

Search for counterexamples or examples of overcoming adversity that go against the restricting conviction.

Rethink the conviction into an enabling and strong assertion.

Practice assertions and positive self-talk that build up the new conviction.

By effectively testing and reevaluating self-restricting convictions, we make space for positive development and open ourselves up to additional opportunities.

Vanquishing Dread: Strategies for Overcoming Obstacles

Fear is a normal human emotion that can either impede our progress or cause us to become paralyzed. It can keep us from seeking after our fantasies, facing challenges, and embracing new open doors. However, we can liberate ourselves from their hold and realize our full potential by comprehending and confronting our fears.

1. The Meaning of Vanquishing Dread

Vanquishing dread is fundamental for self-improvement, achievement, and satisfaction. Dread goes about as a hindrance that restricts our true capacity, impedes progress, and keeps us from carrying on with the existence we want. At the point when we permit dread to direct our activities, we pass up amazing opportunities for learning, development, and change.

Vanquishing dread is critical in light of the fact that it:

Frees us from purposeful limits: Dread frequently originates from self-uncertainty and restricting convictions. By overcoming dread, we challenge these convictions and break free from the imperatives that keep us down.

Individual and expert development: Defying dread requires venturing beyond our usual range of familiarity, facing challenges, and embracing new difficulties. This excursion of development and self-revelation can prompt extraordinary individual and expert accomplishments.

Constructs strength and certainty: Beating dread fortifies our strength as we figure out how to explore vulnerability and face affliction head-on. We gain self-assurance and faith in our abilities with each victory over fear.

Boosts innovation and creativity: Dread can smother our imagination and break our capacity to consider new ideas. Overcoming dread permits us to take advantage of our imaginative potential and embrace creative arrangements.

Opens ways to new doors: At the point when we vanquish dread, we become open to additional opportunities and encounters that were already outside our usual range of familiarity. This extension of chances can be energizing and satisfying.

Types of Dread

Dread can appear in different structures, influencing various parts of our lives. Fears that are common include:

Apprehension about disappointment: the fear of failing to live up to our own or others' expectations, making mistakes, or achieving our objectives

Anxiety toward dismissal: The apprehension about being judged, scrutinized, or dismissed by others can block our eagerness to face challenges and put ourselves out there.

Anxiety toward change: the anxiety that comes from being in a new environment or routine and the fear of the unknown

Apprehension about progress: the anxiety that comes with achieving our goals and the responsibilities and changes that go along with them

Uncertainty dread: the anxiety that comes from having no control over what will happen in the future and the fear of the unknown

We can devise specific strategies to overcome the specific types of fear that prevent us from moving forward.

2. Understanding the Underlying Drivers of Dread

To overcome dread, it is fundamental to comprehend its main drivers. Dread frequently comes from previous encounters, convictions, or an apparent danger to our prosperity. We can gain insight into our fears' origins and address them more effectively by determining their root causes.

To comprehend the underlying causes of fear:

Think about your own set of experiences and previous encounters that might have added to your apprehensions.

Examine any limiting or negative beliefs that are the source of your fears.

Consider cultural or social impacts that might have molded your apprehensions.

Recognize any horrible accidents or molding that have caused dread reactions.

By understanding the main drivers of our feelings of dread, we can foster systems to challenge and conquer them.

3. Developing a Growth Mindset

Developing a growth mindset is an effective strategy for overcoming fear. The belief that our intelligence and abilities can be improved through effort, practice, and education is the growth mindset. It encourages us to approach obstacles with resilience and a willingness to learn and to view challenges as opportunities for growth.

To embrace a development outlook:

Reexamine disappointment as criticism and a chance for learning.

Center around progress and improvement as opposed to prompt achievement.

Accept challenges as opportunities for personal development.

Develop an oddity and long for information.

Challenge self-restricting convictions and supplant them with enabling considerations.

By embracing a development outlook, we shift our point of view on dread and view it as a chance for development and personal growth.

4. Steady Openness and Desensitization

Steady openness and desensitization are methodologies normally used to overcome explicit apprehensions or fears. By slowly exposing ourselves to the article or circumstance that triggers dread, we can desensitize our reaction and fabricate trust in dealing with those circumstances.

to practice desensitization and steady openness:

Start with small, manageable steps that safely and carefully expose you to your fear.

Continuously increase the power or span of openness as you become more agreeable.

Look for help from a specialist, mentor, or care group that has spent significant time tending to explicit feelings of dread or fear.

To manage anxiety during exposure, try relaxation techniques like deep breathing or meditation.

Recognize your progress and celebrate even the smallest victories.

By practicing progressive openness and desensitization, we fabricate certainty and diminish the effect of dread on our lives.

5. Developing Self-Sympathy and Strength

Self-sympathy and strength are essential characteristics for overcoming dread. When we face difficulties or setbacks, self-compassion means treating ourselves with kindness, understanding, and acceptance. Resilience is the capacity to overcome adversity, adapt to change, and persevere in the face of challenges.

To develop self-empathy and strength:

Take care of yourself and give priority to activities that make you feel good.

Indulge yourself with benevolence and understanding during snapshots of dread or self-questioning.

Perceive that difficulties are a characteristic piece of the excursion and a chance for development.

Be surrounded by positive, encouraging people who will lift you up.

Cultivate a positive inner exchange by testing negative self-talk and supplanting it with steady and enabling contemplations.

We acquire the inner strength necessary to confront and conquer our fears by cultivating self-compassion and resilience.

6. Looking for Help and Responsibility

Looking for help and responsibility from others can enormously upgrade our capacity to vanquish dread. Confident companions, tutors, or mentors can give us direction, support, and an outer point of view that assists us in exploring difficulties and remaining propelled.

To look for help and responsibility:

Talk about your worries and difficulties with trusted people who can guide you and support you.

Learn from mentors or coaches who have successfully overcome similar fears or challenges.

Join a community of people who are working toward the same goals, or a support group.

Lay out normal registrations or responsibility meetings with a believed responsibility accomplice.

By looking for help and responsibility, we gain the consolation and direction we need to go up against and overcome our apprehensions.

7. Making a move and Embracing Mental fortitude

Making a move is an essential step toward overcoming dread. We are able to confront our fears, question the limitations we have set for ourselves, and cultivate confidence in our capacity to overcome obstacles when we take action.

to act and embrace mental fortitude:

Separate your objectives into little, reasonable advances.

Start with activities that are within your comfort zone and work your way out of it over time.

Accept discomfort and unpredictability as opportunities for learning and development.

Recognize your bravery and resilience as you work toward your objectives.

Consider past cases where you have confronted dread and effectively defeated it.

We empower ourselves to conquer fear and embrace a life of growth and fulfillment by taking action and embracing courage.

Taking everything into account, overcoming dread is fundamental for self-awareness, achievement, and satisfaction. By grasping the meaning of vanquishing dread, perceiving various kinds of dread, understanding the main drivers, embracing a development mentality, practicing steady openness and desensitization, developing self-empathy and strength, looking for help and responsibility, and making a move, we can beat our feelings of trepidation and open our actual potential. Vanquishing dread is an extraordinary excursion that enables us to carry on with an existence of mental fortitude, development, and satisfaction.

Chapter 5

Perception and Assertion Strategies

Perception and assertions are strong strategies that can decidedly impact our considerations, feelings, and ways of behaving. They permit us to saddle the force of our creative mind and the expressed word to make an ideal reality. By intentionally coordinating our considerations and convictions, we can reconstruct our psyche and fall in line with our objectives and goals. In this chapter, we'll learn about the significance of visualization and affirmations, how they work, and how to use them in real-world situations.

1. Understanding Perception

Perception is the method involved in making striking mental pictures of desired results, encounters, or objectives. To mentally "see," "feel," and "experience" the desired reality as if it has already manifested, it involves engaging our senses and emotions. The reticular activating system (RAS) in our brain, which filters incoming information and directs our attention to what aligns with our mental images, is activated when we visualize, drawing on the power of our imagination.

The meaning of perception lies in its capacity to:

Explain objectives and wants: We can create detailed mental images of our desired outcomes through visualization, which helps us clarify what we really want.

Program the psyche mind: The psyche mind can't separate between genuine and envisioned encounters. By distinctively imagining our ideal reality, we can engrave those pictures into our psyche, impacting our convictions, feelings, and activities.

Boost your drive and focus: Perception assists us with remaining spurred by keeping our objectives more important than anything else to us. It helps us focus better and directs our attention to resources and opportunities that help us visualize.

Boost performance and self-assurance: By intellectually practicing achievement, we foster a feeling of certainty and faith in our capacities. Perception primes our brain and body for progress, working on our presentation of different everyday issues.

Beat limits and hindrances: Representation permits us to intellectually practice beating difficulties and obstructions, setting us up to explore them with certainty and versatility.

2. Procedures for Successful Perception

To rehearse successful perception, think about the accompanying strategies:

Make a reasonable mental picture: Picture your ideal result with striking subtlety, connecting every one of your faculties. Look at the patterns, colors, and textures. Hear the sounds related to your objective. The emotions and sensations associated with achieving it should be felt.

Utilize positive feelings: Mix your representation with positive feelings like bliss, fervor, appreciation, and strengthening. Feelings heighten the effect of representation, making a more grounded association between your longings and the subliminal brain.

Practice consistently: Put aside committed time every day to picture your objectives. Consistency is critical to reconstructing the psyche and mind and supporting the brain processes related to your ideal reality.

Make it genuine and credible. Imagine your ideal result as though it has previously worked out. Feel the feelings of achievement, fulfillment, and appreciation. This helps your psyche and mind acknowledge and put stock in the chance of accomplishing your objectives.

Improve your visualization by reviewing it. Review and improve your visualization as you move closer to achieving your objectives. Change subtleties, consolidate new bits of knowledge, and adjust your psychological picture to mirror any progressions in your desires.

By integrating these procedures into your perception practice, you can upgrade its viability and expand its effect on your psyche and mind.

3. Understanding Affirmations

Positive statements that reflect our desired beliefs, characteristics, or outcomes are called affirmations. They are potent instruments for reprogramming our subconscious mind and directing our thoughts, feelings and actions in the direction of a more optimistic and empowered state. Positive self-talk, self-limiting beliefs and doubts can be replaced with empowering and encouraging thoughts through the use of affirmations.

Affirmations are significant because of their capacity to:

Reprogram the mind's unconscious: Attestations work by redundantly talking about positive explanations that go against negative convictions. This redundancy assists in supplanting old examples with new, enabling convictions.

Enhance self-assurance and self-belief: A feeling of self-worth, confidence, and self-belief is cultivated through affirmations. We build a positive self-image and boost our self-confidence by repeatedly praising our strengths and abilities.

Concentrate on opportunities and possibilities. Affirmations divert our consideration towards valuable open doors, arrangements, and positive results. They assist us with keeping an inspirational outlook and draw in encounters that line up with our certifications.

Conquer self-restricting convictions and questions: Affirmations challenge self-restricting convictions and questions by giving other options and engaging considerations. They hinder negative examples and assist us in embracing more steady convictions about ourselves and our capacities.

Develop strength and positive thinking. By asserting positive articulations, we encourage versatility and hopefulness. Affirmations give consolation, inspiration, and a feeling of inward solidarity to overcome difficulties and mishaps.

4. Techniques for Effective Affirmations

To practice effective affirmations, consider the following techniques:

Use positive language and the present tense. As if your desired reality already exists, frame your affirmations in the present tense. Utilize positive and enabling language that reflects the changes you need to make in your life.

Be explicit and compact. Affirmations should be specific to your objectives and aspirations. Obviously state what you need to accomplish, how you need to feel, or who you need to turn into. Keep your attestations compact and simple to recall.

Always recite affirmations. Recite your confirmations from day to day, in a perfect world, on different occasions each day. Redundancy is vital to reinventing the mind and supporting new convictions.

Connect with your feelings: When you say "yes," try to make yourself feel good about the things you want. As you say your affirmations, feel the joy, gratitude, excitement, and confidence. Affirmations have a greater impact when emotions are involved.

Trust in your confirmations. Move toward your confirmations with conviction. Put your faith in the transformative power of your words. The more you have confidence in your certifications, the more powerful they become.

You can fully utilize the power of affirmations to change your life and reprogram your subconscious mind by incorporating these strategies into your affirmation practice.

5. Combining Visualization and Affirmations

When used together, affirmations and visualizations can have a greater impact and be more effective. When utilized together, these strategies create a strong cooperative energy, as representation gives the psychological symbolism and feelings related to your objectives, while confirmation gives the good convictions and considerations that help your perception.

To combine visualization and affirmations:

Begin by imagining your ideal result meticulously and with close-to-home commitment.

Recite affirmations that bolster the images and emotions you are experiencing as you visualize.

Use affirmative, present-tense statements to speak your affirmations in a manner that is consistent with your visualization.

Draw in your feelings and feel the reality of your certifications as you envision them.

By incorporating representations and confirmations, you adjust your cognizant and subliminal brains, making a strong case for showing your cravings.

6. Practicing Daily Visualization and Affirmation Rituals

To make representation and insistence a predictable piece of your day-to-day existence, think about the accompanying practices:

Every day, set aside time to practice visualization and affirmation.

Set up a serene setting where you can concentrate and use your imagination.

Start with profound breathing or unwinding strategies to focus yourself and calm your brain.

Engage your senses and emotions as you visualize your desired outcome.

Repeat your affirmations several times while speaking with conviction and belief.

Express your gratitude for the manifestations you have visualized and confirmed after your practice.

Throughout the day, maintain an upbeat attitude by reiterating your visualizations and affirmations whenever possible.

You can make visualization and affirmations an integral part of your mindset and increase their effectiveness in shaping your reality by establishing daily rituals for them.

In conclusion, powerful strategies for altering our thoughts, feelings, and actions include visualization and affirmations. We can use our imagination's power to create vivid mental images of our desired reality through visualization. Attestations help us reinvent our psyche by redundantly certifying positive explanations that help our objectives and goals. We can harness the power of our minds to achieve our goals and lead successful lives by incorporating these strategies into our daily lives.

The Art of Visualization: Using Visualization to Create a Vivid Mental Image of Your Desires

Visualization is a potent strategy that enables us to visualize our desires clearly. It includes utilizing our creative mind to make a definite and tangible portrayal of what we need to appear in our lives. Representation takes advantage of the force of the brain and the general rule that good energy attracts good, adjusting our contemplations, feelings, and activities to our ideal results. In this section, we will investigate the craft of perception, figure out its importance, and learn viable systems to bridle its extraordinary power.

1. Understanding the Power of Visualization

Visualization is a skill that has been used for a really long time across different societies and disciplines. It depends on the reason that our contemplations and convictions shape our existence. By deliberately coordinating our considerations and connecting with our creative mind, we can make a psychological picture of our longings and bring them into manifestation.

The capacity that visualization possesses to:

Actuate the psyche mind: Representation discusses straightforwardly our psyche mind, which is answerable for our convictions, feelings, and ways of behaving. We imprint our desires into our subconscious by vividly picturing them, influencing our feelings, thoughts, and actions.

Improve your focus and clarity: We can better understand our desires and goals through visualization. It brings lucidity to our yearnings and coordinates our consideration towards what we need to make in our lives. This engaged consideration permits us to see open doors and assets that line up with our perceptions.

Amplify the law of attraction: According to the law of attraction, like attracts like. By imagining our longings with positive feelings and conviction, we radiate a strong, vivacious vibration that draws in related encounters and valuable open doors into our lives.

Encourage inspiration and motivation: Representation keeps our objectives extremely important to us, propelling and moving us to make a move. It powers our assurance, constancy, and obligation to accomplish our cravings.

Encourage a positive mentality: We can imagine and experience the happiness, contentment, and success associated with our goals through visualization. We are able to overcome obstacles and embrace new possibilities because this positive imagery reshapes our beliefs and cultivates a positive mindset.

2. The Course of Representation

The course of representation includes drawing in our faculties, feelings, and creative mind to make a nitty-gritty mental picture of our cravings. It requires centered consideration and a readiness to suspend doubt, permitting ourselves to submerge ourselves completely in the experience of our representations. We can make our visualizations work better if we follow a methodical approach.

The following are the steps to effective visualization:

Set clear expectations. Start by explaining what you need to appear in your life. Characterize your objectives and wants with particularity and lucidity.

Establish a tranquil and quiet climate. Find a quiet place where you can unwind and concentrate without being interrupted. It could be a comfortable spot in your home or a dedicated meditation area.

Loosen up your body and brain: Take a couple of full breaths and release any pressure in your body. Clear your brain of any diverting contemplations, permitting yourself to enter a loose and responsive state.

Put your senses to use: Start to envision your ideal result, utilizing every one of your faculties. Examine the hues, patterns, and textures that correspond to your desires. Listen to the sounds that you make as you visualize. Feel the sensations and feelings that emerge from accomplishing your objective.

Instill positive feelings: As you imagine, implant your psychological symbolism with positive feelings like euphoria, appreciation, energy, and satisfaction. Feel as though your desire has already come to pass.

Be available in the perception: Put yourself completely into your visualization experience. Be available at the time and draw in the subtleties and feelings of your ideal reality.

Keep faith and belief: Keep your faith in the fulfillment of your goals unwavering. Trust in the force of your perceptions and the course of creation.

Regularly repeat: To reinforce your mental images and beliefs, you should regularly engage in visualization. Consistency is critical to reinventing your mind and conforming to your cravings.

You can increase the transformative power of visualization and make your goals a reality more quickly if you follow these steps and practice it consistently.

3. Enhancing Visualization Techniques

To enhance the effectiveness of your visualization practice, consider incorporating the following techniques:

Representation prearranging: Compose a content or an itemized portrayal of your ideal result. To get a mental picture of your desires, use vivid language and use all of your senses. During your visualization practice, read the script aloud to yourself to reinforce your mental images.

Vision sheets: Make a dream board by gathering pictures, words, and images that address your objectives and wants. Place them in a journal or on a board in a place where you can see them often. To increase the impact of your visualizations, imagine your goals while looking at your vision board.

Directed representation: Support your practice with guided visualization recordings or apps. These assets provide organized representation activities and assist with developing your commitment to the interaction.

Contemplation and unwinding methods: Practice reflection or unwinding strategies before perception to quiet your brain and enter an open state. Methods like profound breathing, moderate muscle unwinding, or directed reflection can assist you in achieving a loose and centered state of perception.

Perception with confirmations: Join perception with positive confirmations that build up your ideal result. Talk about confirmations that line up with your representation, underlining the positive characteristics, convictions, and encounters related to your longings.

By integrating these strategies into your representation practice, you can enhance its effect and make it an all the more useful asset for showing your cravings.

4. Overcoming Challenges and Doubts

During the visualization process, you may encounter obstacles or doubts that prevent you from practicing. It is crucial to address these obstructions to maintain areas of strength for a compelling representation practice.

Self-doubt: Questions might emerge in regards to the possibility or probability of showing your cravings. Remind yourself of your ability to create and the numerous examples of manifestation that exist in the world to put these doubts to rest.

Absence of lucidity: Take some time to clarify your goals if you find it difficult to visualize particular details. Think about what you really need and gain clarity on the points of interest in your ideal result. The more exact and clear your representation, the more grounded its effect.

Impatience: The process of manifestation takes place over time. Be patient and trust the plan of the universe. Discharge any restlessness or connection to the result, permitting your representations to normally unfold.

Reluctance to adapt: In some cases, obstruction emerges while imagining new or different conditions. Recognize any opposition that emerges and investigate the fundamental feelings of trepidation or convictions that might be causing it. Work on letting go of resistance and accepting your visualizations' transformative power.

By tending to these difficulties and questions, you can reinforce your representation practice and beat any obstructions that might impede the manifestation of your longings.

5. Coordinating Perception into day-to-day existence

To expand the effect of perception, incorporating it into your everyday existence and making it a predictable practice is significant. By integrating representation methods into your daily practice, you build up your ideal reality and adjust your contemplations, feelings, and activities to your objectives.

Think about the accompanying techniques to integrate perception into your regular routine:

Morning representation: Start your day with a practice of visualization. Put in no time flat, envisioning your ideal results and establishing an uplifting vibe for the day ahead.

Pauses in visualization: Take short visualization breaks over the course of the day to reconnect with your longings. Take advantage of these breaks to reenergize, refocus, and realign your thoughts with your objectives.

Sleep time representation: End your day with a representation practice before rest. Allowing your subconscious mind to work on manifesting your desires while you sleep is as simple as picturing positive experiences and outcomes.

Reminders for visualization: Utilize viewable signs or updates all through your current circumstance to set off your representation practice. It very well may be an image, an article, or an image that addresses your cravings and fills in as a suggestion for a picture.

Keeping a visual journal: Write about your visualizations in a journal. Record your representations exhaustively, pondering the feelings and sensations related to them. Audit your diary consistently to build up your psychological picture.

By incorporating perception into your regular routine, you create a persistent progression of positive energy and expectation towards the sign of your cravings.

The practice of visualization is a potent strategy for bringing about the life you want. By figuring out the force of representation, following a methodical cycle, upgrading your strategies, beating difficulties, and integrating perception into your day-to-day routine, you can take advantage of the groundbreaking force of your psyche and conform to your ideal reality. Representation is an imaginative and engaging practice that permits you to take part in the co-making of your life effectively. Take hold of the art of visualization and tap into its limitless potential to bring your goals and dreams to life.

Affirmations: Engaging Your Psyche and Programming for Progress

Affirmations are useful assets for shaping our considerations, convictions, and activities. With the intention of reprogramming our subconscious mind and aligning our thoughts with our desired outcomes, we consciously repeat them to ourselves as positive statements. Affirmations have the power to change our perspective, boost our self-esteem, and set us up for success. In this part, we will investigate the specialty of attestations, figure out their importance, and learn down-to-earth systems to bridle their enabling potential.

1. Understanding the Power of Affirmations

Affirmations work on the rule that our contemplations and convictions shape our existence. We begin to rewire our subconscious mind by repeating affirmative statements to ourselves. As a result, negative or self-limiting beliefs are replaced with empowering and supportive ones. Attestations have the capacity to:

Reprogram the mind's unconscious: Our psyche's mind resembles a wipe, retaining and putting away data. We reprogram our subconscious by consistently making positive statements, influencing our thoughts, feelings, and actions.

Change how we see ourselves: Certifications can change our self-discovery by building a positive mental self-portrait. At the point when we confirm our assets, capacities, and value, we develop areas of strength for ourselves and certainty.

Support certainty and self-conviction: Certifications support our certainty by building up sure convictions about ourselves and our capacities. They assist us in overcoming self-doubt and cultivating faith in our ability to accomplish our objectives.

Upgrade inspiration and concentration: Rehashing insistences reliably keeps our objectives more important than anything else to us. They give us inspiration, center, and a feeling of direction, empowering us to remain focused on our goals.

Attract positive experiences:. A powerful energetic vibration emitted by affirmations causes us to attract experiences that are in line with our beliefs. We create a magnetic force that attracts opportunities and resources toward us when we align our thoughts with positivity and success.

2. Making Viable Assertions

Making powerful assertions includes making articulations that resonate with our longings and convictions. Keep in mind the following principles when formulating affirmations:

Utilize the present tense: Write your affirmations in the present tense, acting as though the outcome you want already exists. This assists your psyche and body in lining up with the conviction that what you want is now a reality.

Be explicit and centered: Affirmations should be specific to your goals or desires. Make it crystal clear what it is you want to accomplish or what qualities you want to embody. Particularity gives lucidity and guides your psyche and mind towards showing your goals.

Use a positive tone: Outline your assertions in certain language, stressing what you need as opposed to what you don't need. Center around the thing you are moving towards instead of what you are creating some distance from.

Customize your certifications: Tailor your insistences to reverberate with your novel desires and conditions. Use language that feels true and significant to you, as it will more deeply affect your psyche.

Make them reasonable: Guarantee that your attestations feel reasonable and feasible to you. If you find it hard to believe in an affirmation, you can change it or break it down into smaller steps until you feel like it is achievable.

Emotional use: Include positive feelings and thoughts that are in line with your goals in your affirmations. Feel the delight, appreciation, fervor, or certainty related to accomplishing your objectives as you rehash your certifications.

By following these standards, you can make attestations that reverberate profoundly with your psyche and brain and set yourself up for positive change and achievement.

3. Rehashing and Building up Assertions

Reiteration is vital to the viability of attestations. By reliably rehashing confirmations, you build up sure convictions and condition your brain to embrace new enabling considerations. To get the most out of your affirmations, think about the following methods:

Consistency: Make certifications an everyday practice. Every day, set aside time to repeat your affirmations. Consistency permits your certifications to really infiltrate your mind.

Practice in the morning and evening: Include affirmations in your routines each morning and evening. Set positive goals for the day and keep them in mind before going to bed so that your subconscious mind can work on them at night.

Multiple instances: Rehash your insistences on various occasions during every meeting. An affirmation becomes more ingrained in your subconscious mind the more you repeat it.

Put your senses to use: Engage your senses and emotions when you repeat affirmations. Embrace the feelings evoked by your affirmations and picture yourself living the life you want.

Affirmations in writing: Compose your confirmations in a diary or on sticky notes and spot them where you can see them consistently. Throughout the day, this serves as a reminder and reinforces your positive beliefs.

Assertions in various settings: Affirmations can be incorporated into many aspects of your life. Rehash them during contemplation, while working out, or during calm snapshots of reflection. This broadens your assertion practice and supports positive reasoning in various circumstances.

4. Conquering Opposition and Self-Restricting Convictions

As you embark on your affirmation practice, you might experience obstruction or self-restricting convictions that thwart your advancement. It means a lot to address these difficulties to guarantee the viability of your certifications. Take into account the following methods:

Awareness: Become mindful of self-restricting convictions or negative idea designs that go against your confirmations. Perceive that these convictions are not serving your development and achievement.

Rethink and challenge: Challenge self-restricting convictions by scrutinizing their legitimacy and giving proof that runs against the norm. Change your negative thoughts' reframes into statements that are encouraging and empowering, in line with your affirmations.

Reassurance and reinforcement: Affirmations that directly contradict self-limiting beliefs are a good way to combat them. Rehash certifications that affirm your abilities, value, and potential for progress.

Tolerance and industriousness: Beating well-established convictions takes time and steadiness. Show restraint toward yourself and trust the interaction. Reliably build up certain certifications to supplant self-restricting convictions progressively.

5. Integrating Affirmations into Daily Life

To make affirmations a reliable part of your day-to-day existence, think about incorporating them into different parts of your daily practice. This supports your positive convictions and adjusts your contemplations to your ideal results. Take into account the following methods:

Morning confirmation practice: Recite your affirmations at the beginning of each day. Set an upbeat mood and a goal for the day.

Affirmations during routine exercises: Affirmations should be recited while doing routine things like taking a shower, exercising, or going to work. This permits you to mix inspiration into your day-to-day encounters.

Symbolic reminders: Place obvious prompts or tacky notes with your attestations in noticeable places where you will see them as often as possible. This fills in as an update and builds up certain reasoning over the course of the day.

Affirmations breaks: Repeat affirmations during brief breaks throughout the day. Move back from your undertakings and deliberately realign your contemplations with your confirmations.

Sleep time assertion practice: End your day by recounting confirmations before rest. Reaffirm your belief in your desired outcomes and reflect on the positive experiences of the day.

By incorporating confirmations into your day-to-day routine, you create a ceaseless stream of positive contemplations, convictions, and energy that drives you towards progress.

Affirmations are potent tools for reprogramming your subconscious, empowering your mind, and directing your thoughts toward success. You can unlock the transformative potential of affirmations by comprehending their power, crafting statements that are effective, repeatedly repeating them, overcoming resistance, and incorporating them into your day-to-day life. Affirmations serve as a constant reminder of your intrinsic value, capabilities, and growth potential. Embrace the act of attestations and watch as your outlook moves, your certainty takes off, and your way to progress unfolds before you.

Vision Boards: Tangible Representations of Your Desires

A vision board is a tool that serves as a tangible representation of your desires, goals, and aspirations. It is a montage of pictures, words, and images that portray the existence you need to make. You can engage your creativity, clarify your goals, and bring your dreams to life by making a vision board. Let's take a look at the specialty of vision sheets, grasp their importance, and learn reasonable methodologies to successfully make and use them.

1. Understanding the Power of Vision Boards

The idea behind vision boards is that focused intention and visualization are necessary for achieving our goals. By making a visual portrayal of our objectives and dreams, we enact the imaginative force of our psyche and adjust our considerations, feelings, and activities to achieve our ideal results. Vision boards are effective because they can:

Explain objectives and expectations: We can get a better understanding of our true goals for our lives with the help of vision boards. They act as a visual wake-up call for our objectives and goals, permitting us to remain on track and inspired.

Draw in the psyche mind: Vision sheets discuss straightforwardly with our psyche mind, which is answerable for our convictions and activities. By routinely presenting ourselves to the pictures on our vision board, we program our subconscious with positive and engaging convictions.

Move and inspire: Vision sheets summon feelings, motivation, and inspiration. They keep us motivated and committed to achieving our objectives by acting as a constant reminder of the life we want to live.

Improve imagination and representation: The most common way of making a dream board connects with our inventiveness and creative mind. It improves our capacity to bring our dreams to life by encouraging us to visualize and imagine the life we want.

2. How to Make a Vision Board

Making a vision board is a creative and individual process that lets you tap into your aspirations and desires. Follow these steps toward making your own vision board:

Step 1: Explain your objectives and expectations.

Prior to loading up your vision, find an opportunity to explain your objectives and expectations. Consider various aspects of your life, including your career, relationships, health, and personal development. Distinguish the particular objectives and wants you need to show.

Step 2: Accumulate materials

Accumulate materials for your vision board, including a banner board or material, magazines, printed pictures, markers, paste, scissors, and some other workmanship supplies that impact you. On the other hand, you can make a computerized vision board using web stages or programming.

Step 3: Gather pictures and words.

Flip through magazines or search online for pictures, words, and images that address your objectives and wants. Pick those that impact you on a profound level. Search for pictures that bring out certain feelings and mirror the essence of what you need to show.

Step 4: Collect images and words

Cut out the images and words you want to use, arrange them on your poster board or canvas, and glue them in place. You should experiment with a variety of layouts until you achieve a harmonious and motivating composition. Glue the images and words to your board when you are satisfied.

Step 5: Customize and decorate

Add individual contacts to your vision board to make it uniquely yours. Affirmations written by hand, meaningful quotes, or objects that have symbolic meaning to you can be included. Make your board look better by embellishing it with stickers, markers, or other things.

Step 6: Display your vision board

Place your vision board in a prominent location where you will be able to see it frequently. It may very well be in your room, office, or whatever other space feels important to you. Ensure it is noticeable and effectively open so you can associate with it from day to day.

2. Outfitting the Force of Your Vision Board

When your vision board is made, it turns into a useful asset for showing your cravings. Here are systems to actually use your vision board:

Connect and imagine: Every day, connect with your vision board for a few minutes. Do exercises in visualization in which you mentally enter the scenes on your board. Feel the feelings related to living your ideal reality.

Check in frequently: Set aside some margin to survey your vision board routinely. Consider the pictures, words, and images, and help yourself to remember the objectives and goals they address. Give yourself permission to rekindle the enthusiasm and drive associated with your desires.

Feel the feelings: As you interface with your vision board, drench yourself in the positive feelings that emerge. As if your desires have already come true, feel the joy, excitement, and gratitude. Feelings strengthen the effect of representation and build up the enthusiastic vibration you discharge.

Plan spirited actions: Your vision board isn't only a list of things to get; it's also a source of inspiration. Recognize enlivened moves you can initiate to carry you closer to your objectives. Record these activities and focus on making strides towards their acknowledgment.

Be flexible and open-minded: Having a clear vision is important, but you should also be open to new opportunities and changes along the way. Believe that the universe may have plans for you that are even greater than you can imagine.

Change and improve: Over time, your desires and goals may change. Consistently survey and update your vision board to guarantee it mirrors your ongoing desires. Add new images that are in line with your changing vision and eliminate those that no longer resonate.

3. Intensifying the Force of Advanced Vision Sheets

Not withstanding actual vision sheets, computerized vision sheets offer a helpful and adaptable method for making and drawing in your visual portrayals. When working with digital vision boards, take into consideration the following methods:

Choose an online platform: Select a software program or online platform that lets you make digital collages. Canva, Pinterest, and vision board apps for smartphones and tablets are popular choices.

Gather and curate pictures: Look online for images, quotes, and symbols that help you reach your goals and dreams. To organize your visual content, either save it to your digital platform or create virtual boards.

Tweak and orchestrate: Utilize the devices given by the computerized stage to modify the design, add text, and decorate your advanced vision board. Put the pictures in a way that makes you feel inspired and good-looking.

Set as backdrop or screensaver: Make your computerized vision board effectively available by setting it as your backdrop or screensaver on your electronic gadgets. This guarantees that you associate your vision with different times over the course of the day.

By using computerized vision sheets, you can undoubtedly refresh and get to your visual portrayals, keeping them extremely important to you.

4. Incorporating Your Vision Board Into Your Daily Life

Incorporating your vision board into your daily life will help you get the most out of it. You can incorporate your vision board into your daily life in the following ways:

Morning visualization: Start your day by putting in almost no time associating with your vision load-up. Imagine yourself living your ideal reality and setting positive goals for the day ahead.

Reflection and gratitude: Take time every day to think about your vision, load up, and offer thanks for the signs that are now present in your life. A mindset of abundance and gratitude is developed as a result.

Insistences and mantras: Make assertions or mantras that line up with your vision board and rehash them routinely. Utilize positive proclamations that support your faith in the sign of your longings.

Journaling: Keep a journal and write about your insights, experiences, and progress toward your goals. Think about the feelings and sensations that come with living the life you want.

Solidarity and accountability: Share your vision board with a trusted companion or accomplice who can support you and consider you responsible. Talk about your objectives and desires, and energize each other in your particular processes.

By incorporating your vision board into your day-to-day routine, you support your expectations, adjust your considerations to your cravings, and remain focused on the sign of your fantasies.

In conclusion vision boards are potent instruments for imagining, defining, and bringing your goals to life. Engage your creative mind, activate the law of attraction, and align your thoughts with success by creating a tangible representation of your goals and aspirations. Whether through physical or computerized vision sheets, the key lies in consistently associating with and envisioning your cravings. By incorporating your vision board into your everyday existence and making roused moves towards your objectives, you set yourself up for the manifestation of your fantasies. Embrace the extraordinary force of vision sheets and permit them to push you towards an existence of satisfaction and achievement.

Congratulations! You have journeyed through the pages of "How to Get Exactly What You Want" and discovered the transformative strategies and practices that can empower you to manifest your deepest desires. Throughout this book, we have explored various aspects of understanding, cultivating, and aligning with your desires to create a life of fulfillment and purpose.

May this book serve as a constant reminder that you are capable of creating the life you truly desire. Unlock your desires, trust the process, and let the magic of manifestation unfold in your life. Your dreams are waiting to be realized, and the world is ready to witness the brilliance that emerges from within you.

Now, go forth with confidence and embark on the extraordinary journey of manifesting your desires. Your destiny awaits!